Walking
and
Running

FITNESS, HEALTH & NUTRITION

Walking
and
Running

TIME®
LIFE

by the Editors of Time-Life Books

CONSULTANTS FOR THIS BOOK

Marshall Clark is the Assistant Athletic Director at San Jose State University in California and head coach of the track and field team. He has also coached track and field at the University of Montana and Stanford University, and has trained United States Olympians in the 5000-meter race and the marathon.

Wayne Glusker is a member of the Athletics Congress Race Walk development committee. He is a former 35-kilometer national champion and has been a member of the United States track and field team. Glusker lives in San Jose, California. where he coaches race walking.

William D. McArdle, Ph.D., is a professor in the Department of Health and Physical Education at Queens College of the City University of New York. A Fellow of the American College of Sports Medicine, he is the author of Exercise Physiology: Energy, Nutrition, and Human Performance, Getting in Shape and Nutrition, Weight Control, and Exercise.

Michael A. Motta, M.A., is the chief executive officer of Plus One, a fitness clinic in New York City, He has completed work leading to a doctorate of education in exercise physiology, and he has taught physical education and served as a coach at the State University of New York at Albany.

Allan J. Ryan, M.D., is the editor-in-chief of *Fitness in Business* magazine and the former editor-in-clief of *The Physician and Sportsmedicine* and *Postgraduate Medicine*. He is a former president of the American College of Sports Medicine and a member of many sports medicine and orthopedic organisations.

Bruce Wolfe is a member of the United States orienteering team. He is president of the Bay Area Orienteering Club and has taught orienteering at the University of California at Berkeley, at American River College in Sacramento and to such groups as the Sierra Club and the Boy Scouts.

NUTRITIONAL CONSULTANTS

Ann Grandjean, Ed.D., is Associate Director of the Swanson Center for Nutrition, Omaha, Neb.; chief nutrition consultant to the U.S. Olympic Committee: and an instructor in the Sports Medicine Program, Orthopedic Surgery Department, University of Nebraska Medical Center,

Myron Winick. M.D., is the R.R. Williams Professor of Nutrition, Professor of Pediatrics, Director of the Institute of Human Nutrition, and Director of the Center for Nutrition, Genetics and Human Development at Columbia University College of Physicians and Surgeons. He has served on the Food and Nutrition Board of the National Academy of Sciences and is the author of many books, including *Your Personalized Health Profile*.

This edition published in 2005
by the Caxton Publishing Group
20 Bloomsbury Street, London WC1B 3JH

Under license from Time-Life Books BV.

Cover Design: Open Door Limited, Rutland UK

Editor: Charles L. Mee Jr..
Editor: Thomas Dickey
Senior Editor: William Dunnett
Test Editor: Linda Epstein
Associate Editor: Mary Crowley
Chief of Research: Carney W. Mimms III
Copy Editor: Robert Hernandez
Contributing Editors: Jacqueline Damian, Jane Schechter
Art Director. Judith Henry
Associate Art Director: Francine Kass
Designer: Sara Bowman
Still Life and Food Photographer: Steven Mays
Contributing Photographer: David Madison
Photo Stylist: Leah Lococo
Test Kitchen Director. Grace Young
Recipe Editor: Bonnie J. Slotnisck

Title: Walking and Running

ISBN: 1 84447 167 5

This book is not intended as a substitute for the advice of a physician. Readers who have or suspect they may have specific medical problems, especially those involving muscles and joints, should consult a physician before beginning any programme of strenuous physical exercise.

CONTENTS

CHAPTER ONE

The Premier Exercises

Varied, convenient, suitable for virtually anyone — and with a multitude of benefits

As forms of exercise, walking and running are no longer fads: millions of people have discovered the physical and psychological dividends of these activities and have made them a permanent part of their lives. It is not difficult to understand why: both exercises are suitable for any age, they can be performed alone or in a group, they require no special skills, and you need not join a club, use machinery or purchase special equipment (other than proper shoes) to enjoy them. You can step out of the front door and take off. For people who have never undertaken an exercise programme, walking and running are excellent ways to get started — and this book will show you the safest, most effective ways to design a programme for either exercise. If you already walk or run, you will find information to help you hone your technique, upgrade your programme and, most important, add variety to keep your regimen invigorating mentally and physically. The specific fitness benefits of walking and running are spelt out in this chapter.

Why are walking and running such good exercises?
Both will effectively develop cardiovascular endurance — the most important component of overall fitness — because they are aerobic exercises: that is, they develop the heart's capacity to deliver oxygenated blood to the working muscles and simultaneously improve their capacity to use this oxygen. Aerobic exercise requires continuous, rhythmical movement of at least 50 per cent of your body's muscle mass. To condition your heart effectively, that exercise must raise your heart rate above 65 per cent of its maximum capacity for at least 20 minutes. Walking and running use all the major muscles in your legs, which comprise about four times the muscle mass of your arms. When these muscles work, they require oxygen from the blood, which makes your heart pump faster to deliver that blood. Like any other muscle, the heart becomes stronger in response to having to work harder, and the more powerful your heart, the more blood it pumps per beat; consequently, the less often it has to pump to deliver the necessary blood to your muscles.

Many benefits are attributed to regular aerobic exercise. The most important result is reducing the risk of cardiovascular disease, the leading cause of mortality in the United Kingdom and Europe. Regular exercise has been shown to increase the pumping capacity of the heart and possibly the diameter of coronary arteries, while also lowering the blood concentrations of triglycerides (fatty acids) and low-density lipoproteins, or LDLs, the "bad" cholesterol that can cause plaque to accumulate on the walls of arteries. Regular exercise also appears to raise the level of high-density lipoproteins, the "good" HDLs, which carry cholesterol to the liver to be broken down.

Among the other benefits associated with aerobic exercise are a reduction in the risks of osteoporosis, hypertension and diabetes, and an enhanced ability to maintain optimal body weight. Psychological tests have shown that those who start exercising become more self-confident and emotionally stable. In addition, regular physical activity — even if it is not strenuous enough to raise your heart rate to 65 per cent of its maximum — has recently been shown to reduce the risk of stroke, respiratory disease, cancer, and even death.

Are walking and running better for your health than other forms of aerobic exercise?
No. You can derive similar fitness and health benefits from cycling, rowing, aerobics, skipping, swimming, cross-country skiing and any other activity in which you move the large skeletal muscles, particularly the leg muscles, for a continuous period of time. But many people find that walking and running are more convenient than other activities because — by their very simplicity and accessibility — they are easy to begin and to maintain on a regular basis.

Most people, even those who have been completely sedentary, can walk to improve their fitness. And with a minimum amount of effort

The Biomechanics of Walking and Running

At first glance, the biomechanics of walking and running seem much the same: each foot alternately stays in contact with the ground and propels your body forwards. However, as you move from walking to running, you change the biomechanics of your stride significantly, as shown below.

The walking gait can be divided into two phases: stance and swing. The stance portion consists of the initial foot strike and the movement of the legs to the point where your other foot makes contact with the ground. The swing portion brings your leg back to the foot-strike position.

In running (bottom), the same basic motions make up stance and swing, but the stance phase is shortened because your pace is faster. Also, the moment in the walking cycle when both feet are on the ground is replaced by the float phase in which the body is propelled through the air.

Walking

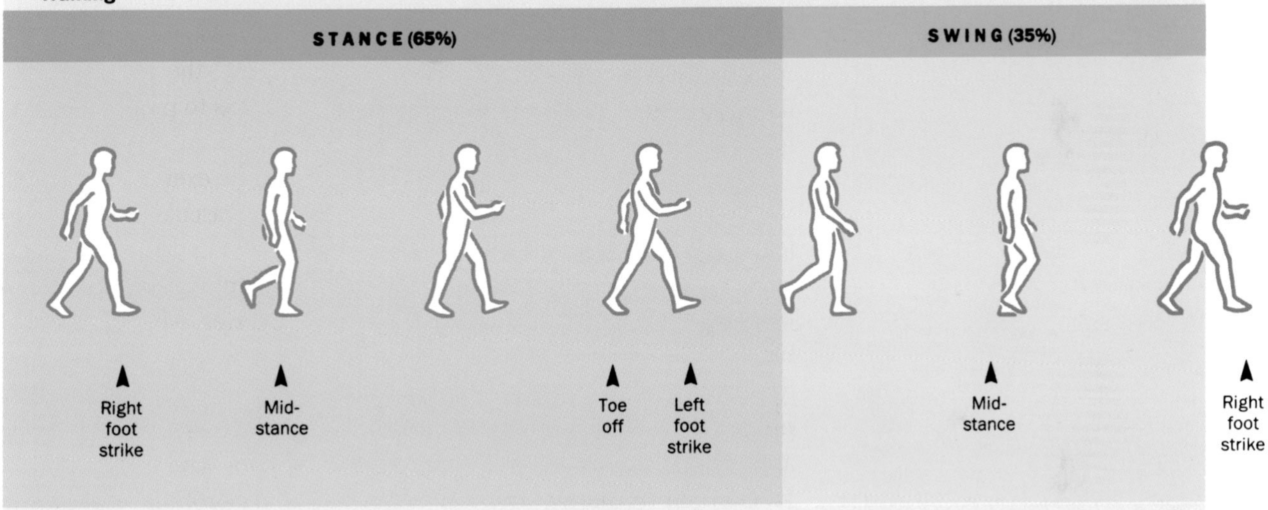

STANCE (65%)				SWING (35%)	
Right foot strike	Mid-stance	Toe off	Left foot strike	Mid-stance	Right foot strike

Running

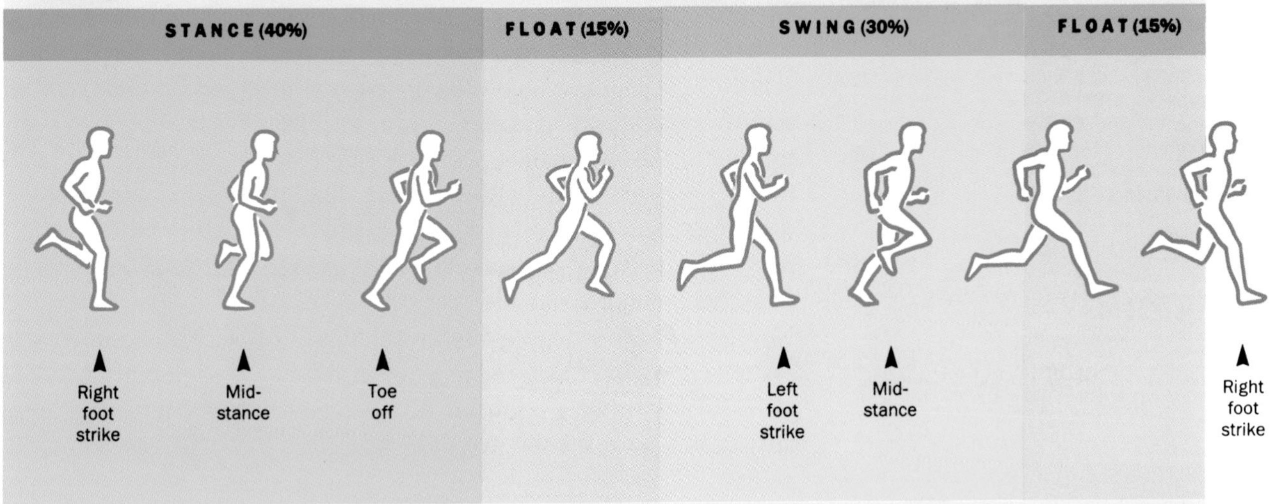

STANCE (40%)			FLOAT (15%)	SWING (30%)		FLOAT (15%)
Right foot strike	Mid-stance	Toe off		Left foot strike	Mid-stance	Right foot strike

Energy for Speed vs. Distance

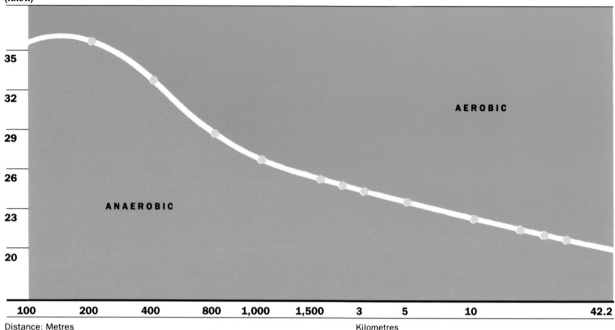

Speed (km/h)

ANAEROBIC

AEROBIC

35
32
29
26
23
20

100   200   400   800   1,000   1,500   3   5   10   42.2

Distance: Metres   Kilometres

Fuel for exercise is provided by the body's two energy systems: aerobic (meaning "with oxygen") and anaerobic ("without oxygen"). The chart above plots the speeds maintained by elite athletes in a variety of running events, from sprints to the marathon, and the arc of this performance curve suggests the contribution of each energy system. The short, intense sprints on the left are predominantly anaerobic, while the longer endurance runs are mainly aerobic. At the 800 to 1,000-metre zone, each system provides an equal amount of energy. And neither system is ever totally dominant; there is always some contribution, however small, by the other.

and training, most people can also run. To ensure that you will keep exercising throughout your life, experts advise that your workout programme be simple: the less organization, equipment, expense or travelling you need to do, the better. In addition, your exercise programme should somehow be incorporated into your everyday activities. The less apparatus or preparation you need, and the less you depend on going to a class or health club, the better. Recent data suggest that people who engage in informal exercise on their own — such as walking and running — are most likely to continue with their training in the long term.

Many experts also believe that a lifetime exercise programme should have as much diversity as possible. No routine fulfils this requirement better than walking and running. Both activities can be practised indoors or outside, and you can vary the kind of walking and running you do — from exercise walking to hiking and orienteering, from race walking and jogging to sprinting, "fun running" (racing without pressurizing yourself to win) and even competing in a marathon — as this book will show you.

Is running better than walking?

The answer to this question depends on what your goals and preferences are, and which activities best fit into your everyday life. While it may be more difficult to raise your heart rate to your training range — that is, between 65 and 85 per cent of its maximum — by walking, many people find that walking is easier to incorporate into their daily lives. Walking to work, or part of the way to work, is an option for many people who cannot change their clothes when they arrive, as they would probably need to do if they ran to work. According to the recent large-scale Canada Fitness Survey, the convenience of walking has made it the most popular exercise of all. And in Britain, more than eight million people regularly go walking for exercise.

Because the impact force of running is two to three times body weight — much more than the impact force of walking — runners are somewhat more likely to be injured than walkers, and running can be too stressful for some out-of-shape beginners. However, running is a tremendously popular activity: in the United Kingdom, an estimated one million people run at least once a week. Some runners find that competition motivates them to stick with an exercise programme, and the existence of numerous races makes them prefer running to walking for their regular workouts.

The question of whether to walk or run is also related to another question: is cardiovascular fitness your goal, or simply physical activity? Running is a powerful conditioner for the cardiovascular system; for many people, walking is less intense. Experts disagree on which is best for you. However, one major study by a research institute in Dallas, Texas, followed more than 10,000 men for a little longer than eight years and correlated their exercise and activity habits with mortality from all causes. Called the Aerobics Center Longitudinal Study, this research found that both running and walking probably have about equal benefit for increasing your lifespan.

How are fitness and activity measured?
Fitness can be measured by the volume of oxygen you can consume while exercising at your maximum capacity. This is your VO_2max. Those who are more fit have higher VO_2max values and can exercise more intensely than those who are not as well conditioned. Numerous studies show that you can increase your VO_2max by working out at an intensity that raises your heart rate to between 65 and 85 per cent of its maximum for at least 20 minutes three to five times a week.

Your activity level is more difficult to measure. Researchers generally have to rely on reports submitted by study subjects. In the Harvard Alumni Study of nearly 17,000 male graduates in the United States, subjects reported how many city blocks they walked, how many stairs they climbed, the types of sports they engaged in and the time they spent on these activities each week. The researchers assigned energy costs for each activity — 56 calories for walking seven city blocks, for instance, and 28 calories for climbing 70 stairs. Those who were active and burnt more calories suffered less from cardiovascular disease and other illnesses than did their sedentary peers; the active ones also tended to live longer. Furthermore, those who expended at least 2,000 calories per week on physical activity had the greatest overall reduction in the risk of death.

How much should you walk or run each week to increase your chances of living longer?

Since you burn approximately 100 calories per 1,500 metres when you run, you will expend 2,000 calories if you run 30 kilometres a week, thus putting yourself in the lower risk category for premature death. Most people could cover 30 kilometres a week if they ran for about 30 to 40 minutes per day for five days. And brisk walking for at least 30 kilometres per week will also fulfil the requirement for burning 2,000 calories, although this may require walking from five to eight hours per week. Although many people may not be able to accumulate this amount of walking time on a weekly basis, the findings of the Harvard study also showed that simply walking 15 kilometres a week will significantly reduce your chances of developing heart disease.

Is strenuous walking enough to improve fitness?

Many people wonder if walking (other than race walking) is strenuous enough to produce any aerobic benefits or help them lose weight. To test this, researchers at the University of Massachusetts asked 271 males and females aged 30 to 69 to walk as fast as they could on a treadmill for the equivalent of 1,500 metres. While the subjects walked, the researchers monitored their heart rates and found that at least 86 per cent of all the females, regardless of age, and 81 per cent of the males over 50 years old were able to walk vigorously enough to maintain a heart rate of 70 per cent of maximum. The researchers found, however, that many of the younger, fitter males were not able to attain their target heart rates and that, for them, walking was not intense enough to ensure an aerobic benefit.

On the other hand, it may not be necessary to exercise at such an intensity that you achieve your target heart rate of 65 to 85 per cent of your maximum. (To find your target heart rate, see page 17.) Many benefits attributed to training at high levels of intensity can also be achieved by training at lower levels. Researchers at the University of Pittsburgh asked 10 sedentary men to walk briskly on a treadmill for 20 minutes. They found that this level of exercise, which raised the subjects' heart rates to an average of 50 per cent of maximum, raised their blood levels of HDL cholesterol significantly without raising the overall cholesterol level. Research has also shown that lower-intensity exercise will increase aerobic fitness if the duration of the activity is sufficient. In essence, if the intensity of your exercise session is reduced, lengthen the time you work out.

In any case, there are many ways to make walking intense enough to raise your heart rate into its target zone and to expend enough calories to make you lose weight. These include hill walking, carrying hand weights and race walking *(see Chapter Two)*.

T*ake the following necessary precautions to minimize the chance of injury:*

• *Be sure that you wear shoes specifically designed for walking or running.*

• *Warm up before you engage in any vigorous exercise.*

• *Stretch after warming up or exercising to maintain flexibility.*

• *Establish and maintain an adequate training base and increase your exercise gradually.*

• *Be sure that you are properly trained before you enter competitions or events.*

• *Drink plenty of fluids when exercising on warm or hot days.*

If running is good for you, why are runners injured so often?

While it is true that runners get hurt, their injuries are usually minor. A few days of rest or reducing your distance or the intensity of your workout generally results in a complete recovery. Some exercise physiologists believe that the risk of injury to runners is exaggerated. They point out that statistics regarding injury rates for runners and others who exercise are quite meaningless because the studies have failed to use control groups.

In one study that did use a control, researchers asked two groups of individuals — one group that ran and performed other exercises, and the control group that was inactive — whether they had sustained a bone, muscle or joint injury within the past year that had caused them to stop exercising or curtail other activities for at least a week. The researchers found only a 10 per cent difference in injury rates between the two groups. In another study of 3,000 injured runners and non-runners who sought medical care, researchers found only a 2 per cent difference in injury rates between the two groups. Although the runners had more knee problems than those who did not run, injury rates were similar for both groups for the hip, ankle, foot, back, elbow and shoulder areas.

Are you in danger of a heart attack if you run too hard?

The concern that running can place too much stress on the heart was sparked off in 1984 by the death of marathon runner and best-selling author James Fixx, who died of a heart attack while running. A study published in 1987 reported 36 cases of heart attack or sudden death in marathon runners worldwide. These deaths dispelled a widely held notion that anyone fit enough to run a marathon, an extremely demanding 42.2-kilometre road race, simply could not be suffering from life-threatening coronary artery disease.

However, the same study found that 71 per cent of the victims had experienced symptoms of cardiovascular disease but had ignored them, just as James Fixx was reported to have done. He had, it seems, refused to have a complete physical examination or to take a stress test, so he was unaware of his condition. Indeed, Fixx had many risk factors that predisposed him to heart disease, and he might have lived an even shorter life had he not been a runner.

In the general population, exercise-related deaths are actually quite rare: one study of active males whose ages ranged from 30 to 64 revealed that the risk of their dropping dead while running was one in 7,620. And although physically active people have a slightly higher chance of dying from a heart attack while they are exercising than when they are not, their overall risk of sudden death is 60 per cent less than that of sedentary men.

Among cardiologists and physical therapists, walking and running are now widely accepted as healthy exercises for recovering cardiac patients. As long as patients are carefully monitored and do not have

The Training Zone

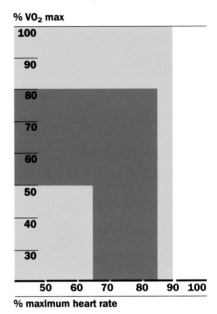

% VO_2 max

% maximum heart rate

To obtain aerobic benefits from walking and running, you must exercise at your target heart rate, which varies with your age and falls within a zone ranging from 65 to 85 per cent of your maximum heart rate. As the chart above shows, this training zone can be correlated to maximum oxygen uptake, or VO_2max, a precise measurement of fitness that expresses the amount of oxygen your body can take in and use during one minute of intense exercise. (Instructions for determining your target heart rate are given on page 17.)

symptoms that could indicate a potential problem, they can increase their training if they wish. In fact, at least three heart-transplant recipients have completed marathons.

How can you prevent walking and running from becoming monotonous routines?

About 50 per cent of people who are sufficiently concerned about their health to begin exercise programmes drop out within six months to a year — even cardiac patients, who stand to benefit the most from exercise, drop out at a rate as high as 70 per cent. Studies show that those who withdrew from exercise programmes reported that their workout routines were boring or the facilities were expensive and inconvenient. If you walk or run, expense and inconvenience will not be problems; as this book shows, both exercises can be varied sufficiently to help keep your interest and motivation from flagging.

A study of 1,299 patients at the Cooper Clinic in Dallas, Texas, is a case in point. It showed that at the first of four clinic visits, only 50 per cent of the subjects were active. By the fourth visit, 96 per cent of those who were active initially were still exercising; of those who were inactive initially, 75 per cent were exercising. Part of the clinic's high success rate may be the result of its repeated testing of patients, which is thought to motivate them to improve their fitness.

As an alternative to the motivation provided by a clinic's frequent testing, you may find that competition helps you to stick to a training programme. Generally, if you train to race you will be improving your fitness along with your performance. It is not necessary to train at a competitive athlete's level to be fit; you can take advantage of many techniques that athletes use — such as running intervals on a track or "fartlek" training, or "speed play" — to enhance your enjoyment of exercise as well as your performance (see Chapter Three). Entering races and fun runs can thus become a useful tool for self-evaluation and motivation.

Should you engage in other exercises and activities in addition to walking or running?

There are many aspects of fitness — for instance, strength, speed, endurance, aerobic fitness, co-ordination, flexibility, balance, agility and the ratio of lean-to-fat body tissue. Walking and running, while they are excellent aerobic and endurance conditioners that also help reduce body fat, may not build all other aspects of fitness with equal effectiveness. Many runners and walkers, therefore, would benefit from flexibility training and upper body workouts to develop strength and upper body muscle endurance.

The walking and running chapters (Chapters Two and Three) offer stretching routines to increase flexibility and joint range of motion. Chapter Four includes an upper body strength-training workout that is specifically designed to condition walkers and runners.

The Training Effect

The first link in the oxygen-delivery system to be affected by exercise is the lungs. When you begin to exercise aerobically, your ventilation increases exponentially for the first few minutes, then settles into a fairly steady elevated state that lasts as long as you continue the activity.

In fact, the lungs of an untrained person deliver more oxygen than his unconditioned skeletal muscles and heart can use. As a result, the heart and other muscles are the limiting factors in performance, as suggested by the illustration above.

Ultimately, though, the situation is reversed *(below)*, since the skeletal muscles and heart make far more significant adaptations to exercise than do the lungs, which are capable of only modest alterations. The most profound changes are in the skeletal muscles; their rich network of capillaries expands, along with the number of microscopic energy factories called mitochondria. Next is the heart, which pumps more blood. Thus, in a highly fit person, the lungs may be the limiting factor in improved performance.

How to Design Your Own Programme

There are three keys to designing a satisfying exercise programme: know what your goals are; choose an activity that you enjoy and can work into your daily schedule; and get started properly. The latter is especially important: studies show that the most common mistake that people make is to start an exercise programme too aggressively. If you try to do too much too soon, you are likely to tire quickly, become discouraged and increase your chances of getting injured.

The questions and answers on these two pages will help you to evaluate your current level of fitness and your exercise goals; the following five pages show how to develop a walking or running schedule that is comfortable and gradually progressive. This section also contains guidelines for choosing equipment and a chart for preventing injuries.

What shape are you in?

1 How active are you?

Your general level of fitness hinges on three components: how often, how long and how vigorously you perform an activity. To be minimally fit, you should exercise at least three times a week for 20 minutes each time. Equally important, the exercise should raise your pulse and breathing rate for a sustained period — that is, it should be aerobic. Activities that involve bursts of strength or speed — such as weightlifting or tennis — are predominantly anaerobic, and while they may provide some aerobic benefits, they are not nearly as good for building cardiovascular fitness as walking or running.

2 How fit are your heart and lungs?

The ability of your cardiovascular system to sustain an endurance activity such as walking or running is the primary indicator of fitness. The most accurate way to judge this ability is with a laboratory test in which you run on a treadmill or ride a bicycle while your oxygen consumption is measured. Such an exercise stress test is not usually necessary if you are under 35 and in good health. But if moderate activity — for instance, walking up a flight of stairs — makes you out of breath, then you probably have a low level of cardiovascular endurance. If that is the case, start your exercise programme by walking or by following the guidelines for running beginners on pages 20 and 21. If you have not exercised regularly for over a year, if you are over 35 or if you are at any risk of heart disease, you should consult your doctor before beginning an exercise programme.

3 Are you overweight?

Excessive fat detracts from your appearance and contributes to a variety of health problems, including high cholesterol levels. The extra weight also places a burden on virtually all of the body's organs, especially the heart, as well as on the joints and muscles.

Studies have shown that many obese people do not eat significantly more than thin individuals, but are much less active. A crucial part of any weight-loss programme, therefore, is adding activities to your daily life that increase calorie expenditure substantially. The charts on pages 19 and 20 show the number of calories you burn while walking and running, and suggest workout guidelines that will allow you to lose significant amounts of fat.

4 Have you ever sustained a stress injury?

Stress injuries are caused by overloading muscles, ligaments and tendons over a period of days or weeks. The damage may have no obvious cause, but it often results in inflammation of the stressed tissues, accompanied by such symptoms as pain or swelling in muscles or tendons, and stiffness or pain in joints. (The chart on pages 22-23 cites the causes of specific injuries.) If you have tried running and given it up because of a stress injury, you can guard against re-injury by wearing proper shoes and building up your training programme gradually. (For tips on choosing shoes, see pages 24-25.)

5 Do you want to walk or to run?

Theroretically, the most effective exercise is the one that promotes the highest VO$_2$max — the indicator of how efficiently your system processes oxygen for energy. But unless you already train at high intensity, your heart is likely to benefit from walking as well as running. It is most important to choose an activity that is accessible to you and that you enjoy — studies show these two qualities provide the best insurance for sticking to an exercise. If you decide to pursue a walking programme, you can use hand weights to increase the intensity of the exercise as your level of fitness improves. Walkers can also progress to running, while many runners will enjoy walking variations such as hiking and orienteering, covered in Chapter Two.

6 If you already walk or run, do you also perform any other exercises regularly?

While walking and running help build muscular strength and endurance in your lower body, they contribute little to keeping your upper body strong, firm and flexible. Strength and flexibility help you perform all sorts of tasks with greater ease and agility and also reduce the chances of injury to muscles and joints. If you do not at present perform a workout for your upper body, the strengthening exercises in Chapter Four should become an integral part of your weekly exercise regimen.

How hard to train

The pace at which you walk or run is of vital importance in achieving optimal aerobic benefits. Researchers have determined that your heart rate can serve as a guide to exercise intensity, and have devised a formula for calculating the rate that you should aim for during an aerobic workout.

To find your target heart rate, first determine your maximum heart rate, which is 220 minus your age. Multiply that figure first by 65 per cent and then by 85 per cent. After warming up, your heart rate during exercise should be somewhere between the two numbers you have calculated. If you are 35 years old, for example, your heart rate should reach at least 120 beats per minute and not exceed 157 beats. Most people will find that after several months, exercising in the 70 to 80 per cent range is comfortable.

To find your heart rate while exercising, stop briefly to take your pulse at the main artery in your wrist. Count the number of beats for 10 seconds, and multiply by six.

Walking Workouts

To derive aerobic benefits from walking, you need only increase the pace at which you usually walk. Normal walking is an efficient activity that does not take much energy, but as you walk faster, you become less efficient and burn more calories.

As the chart opposite shows, oxygen consumption and caloric expenditure rise steadily as you increase your speed from 3 kilometres per hour to 7 kilometres per hour. At even faster speeds, the caloric expenditure rises so quickly — in part, because the efficiency of the walking stride starts to decline — that researchers have found it is not possible to predict accurately how many calories you can burn by walking at these speeds.

However, you do not have to walk at top speed to get a good workout. The lower chart on the opposite page shows that swinging your arms vigorously while carrying hand weights can be adequate exercise even at a normal walking pace.

Exercise walking is not the only way to walk for fitness. You can also get a good workout from hiking over rugged terrain, orienteering through the wilderness with a map and compass as your guide, or race walking, a competitive sport. The guide below summarizes these forms of walking and refers you to pages that describe them in greater detail.

A Walking Guide

EXERCISE WALKING	ORIENTEERING	HIKING	RACE WALKING
To walk for exercise, use a thrusting stride and vigorous arm swings to increase the number of calories burnt. Carry 0.5 to 1-kilogram hand weights to boost the intensity of your workouts.	Cross-country hiking using a map and compass is called orienteering. This can be a competitive activity with formal meets and championships, or simply a way to navigate unknown territory.	Hiking means trail walking, often carrying a backpack. Hiking is most frequently a weekend or holiday activity that can add variety to your regular workout. Its challenges come primarily from difficult terrain.	The fastest and most energetic form of walking is race walking. A competitive sport and an Olympic event, race walking is an excellent fitness-building activity and can be an aid in weight control.
Pages 38-45	Pages 54-59	Pages 52-53	Pages 46-51

Calories Burnt by Walking

KM/H	BODY WEIGHT IN KILOGRAMS				
	55	65	75	85	95
3	2.5	2.8	3.1	3.3	3.7
4	3.1	3.5	3.8	4.2	4.5
5	3.7	4.2	4.5	5.0	5.4
6	4.3	4.9	5.3	5.8	6.4
7	4.9	5.5	6.1	7.0	7.5

Approximate caloric expenditure per minute based on walking speed and body weight.

Increasing the Effort

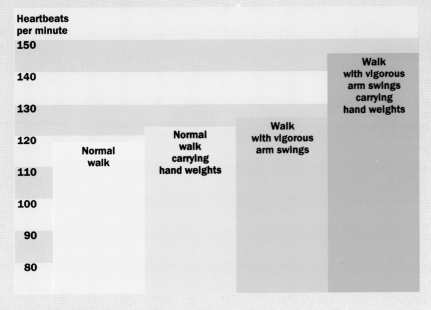

The chart on the left compares ways in which you can increase the intensity of walking. Based on a study of college students, it shows that either carrying 1-kilogram hand weights or swinging your arms vigorously will probably only elevate your heart rate slightly. However, the subjects who carried hand weights and swung their arms vigorously at the same time raised their heart rates by over 20 per cent.

Running Workouts

First and foremost, running should be fun. If you run to fulfil someone else's notion of what you should be doing, you will not enjoy it. The charts on the opposite page give three sample running schedules; however, you need not adhere to them strictly. Instead, use them as guidelines.

If you are just starting out as a runner, begin by jogging two or three times a week for 10 to 15 minutes. Do not worry about the distance you run; work on increasing your time gradually, building up to four days a week. Pick one day at the weekend to put in a longer run.

Once you have established a beginner's schedule and maintained it for a month or more, graduate to an intermediate level such as the one shown on the opposite page. Increase your training programme until you run six days a week for at least 30 minutes a day, with an hour run at the weekend.

If you want to begin training at a more advanced level, start running for distance. Measure the length of specific routes in your car. Do easy runs of 8 kilometres and over, and harder runs for shorter distances, on alternate days of the week. Do a long run at the weekend and be sure to take one day off, as the bottom chart on the right shows. The chart on this page tells how many calories you burn running at various speeds.

Calories Burnt by Running

KM/H	BODY WEIGHT IN KILOGRAMS				
	55	65	75	85	95
8	7.1	8.3	9.4	10.7	11.8
9	8.1	9.8	11.0	12.6	14.4
10	9.1	10.8	12.2	13.6	15.3
11	10.2	11.8	13.1	14.7	16.6
12	11.2	12.8	14.1	15.6	17.6
13	12.1	13.8	15.0	17.0	18.9
14	13.3	15.0	16.1	17.9	19.9
15	14.3	15.9	17.0	18.8	20.8
16	15.4	17.0	18.1	19.9	21.9

Approximate caloric expenditure per minute based on running speed and body weight.

Sample Workouts

GETTING STARTED
Running continuously without regard for speed

M	Tu	W	Th	F	Sa	Su
20 min.	OFF	20 min.	OFF	20 min.	OFF	30 min.

INTERMEDIATE SCHEDULE
Running continuously at 10-13 km/h

M	Tu	W	Th	F	Sa	Su
30 min.	30 min.	30 min.	30 min.	45 min.	OFF	60 min.

PRECOMPETITIVE SCHEDULE
Varying workout intensity on alternate days

M	Tu	W	Th	F	Sa	Su
5-8 km HARD	8 km EASY	5-8 km HARD	8 km EASY	5-8 km HARD	OFF	13-16 km EASY

HARD: A pace that works your heart at 75 to 85 per cent of your maximum heart rate.
EASY: A pace that works your heart at 60 to 75 per cent of your maximum heart rate.

Common Running and Walking Complaints

Most runners and many walkers occasionally experience discomfort or pain due to injury. Many of these are stress, or overuse, injuries, the result of repeated microtrauma caused by intensive running and walking. If you are injured, reduce your training or stop altogether. Ice the affected area and keep it elevated for as long as you experience pain and swelling. If pain persists, or if you have any questions about your injury, consult a doctor.

COMPLAINT/SYMPTOMS	PREVENTION AND RECOVERY TIPS
Achilles tendinitis Tightness or a burning sensation in the area from the lower calf to the heel, particularly when rising from bed	Be sure to warm up thoroughly and stretch frequently, as shown on pages 35 and 67. Strengthen your calves, as shown on page 34. Take it easy when you run or walk uphill. If pain persists or is disabling, consult a doctor.
Ankle sprain Acute pain, most severe when standing or walking, and swelling of the ankle	Apply ice immediately after spraining, elevate the leg and use compression. Ice your ankle as often as possible for the first few days following your injury. If your ankle cannot bear weight, see a doctor.
Black toenails A sometimes painful condition resulting from blood collecting underneath the nails, which fall off if untreated	A doctor will puncture the toenail to release the blood and prevent loss of the nail. To avoid recurrences, make sure that your shoes have enough toe room.
Blisters Most common in the summer when perspiration increases friction between your feet and shoes, irritating skin	Clean the area round the blister carefully and puncture through the adjacent skin with a sterile needle to drain off the fluid. If the blister becomes infected, remove the top of it completely. To avoid blisters, rub petroleum jelly over the balls of your feet, your heels and other blister-prone spots.
Chafing Redness and discomfort of the skin, usually on the inner thighs or nipples	Friction between the skin and clothing or between skin rubbing against skin causes this problem. Rub petroleum jelly on troublesome areas, or wear soft, non-binding clothing. Nylon fabric may also help.
Cuboid bone displacement Pain or tenderness on the outside of the ankle that is difficult to pinpoint, resulting in an inability to push off the toes	This is an acute injury that can occur suddenly, especially after running or walking over rugged terrain. If pain persists, see a chiropodist.
Delayed muscle soreness Sore, stiff muscles a day or two after exercise, such as a race or excessive downhill running	Warm up and stretch adequately before exercise. Running or walking will relieve the soreness, but be sure to exercise at a lower intensity.
Dizziness A feeling of faintness caused by a sudden drop in blood pressure, especially after standing up from a seated position	This is often a symptom of overtraining. Cut back slightly on your exercise programme. If you feel dizzy while running or walking on a warm day, however, you may be dehydrated. Stop immediately and drink plenty of cool water. If dizziness persists, consult a doctor.
Groin strain Pain or tightness on the inside of the thighs, resulting in a loss of stability and control as you swing your legs forwards	Perform gentle stretches for the adductor muscles, such as the exercise shown on page 69. Warm up sufficiently before running or walking.

COMPLAINT/SYMPTOMS	PREVENTION AND RECOVERY TIPS
Hamstring pull Pain, tightness or swelling in the back of the thigh, forcing a shortened stride that is lacking in power	Be sure to warm up before exercising and take extra time to stretch your hamstrings and quadriceps *(see pages 35, 36 and 68)*.
Heel spur Pain and swelling just under the heel bone, sometimes accompanied by tenderness and pain along the bottom of the foot	Stretch and strengthen the calf muscles, as shown on pages 34-35 and 67. Make sure your shoes have adequate arch support.
Iliotibial band pain Discomfort, tenderness or burning sensation on the outside of the knee, sometimes radiating up the thigh	Reduce the distance and workout intensity, and avoid hills and excessive running in one direction on roads with a gradient. Make sure your shoes prevent excessive pronation of your feet.
Lower back pain Back muscle spasms or pain when bending or stretching your back	Strengthen your abdominal muscles, as shown on pages 120-123. Also, perform the lower back stretch, as shown on page 69.
Neuroma Numbness, tingling, pain or burning sensation between or under the toes	Make sure your shoes allow adequate toe room and have good forefoot cushioning. If pain persists, see a chiropodist.
Runner's knee Pain behind or round the kneecap	Avoid sprinting and excessive workouts on hills. Make sure your shoes prevent excessive pronation of your feet.
Sciatica Pain or cramping in the thighs and buttocks; tingling or numbness on the outside of the feet and toes	Avoid hill workouts. Be sure to perform hamstring and lower back stretches *(see pages 36 and 69)*. If pain persists, consult a doctor.
Shin splints Discomfort, tenderness or burning pain along the shins	Warm up gradually, and run or walk on soft surfaces. If pain is acute, stop altogether for a few days. If pain persists, it may be due to a stress fracture; consult a doctor.
Side stitch Cramps, usually in the upper right abdominal area, when running or walking	Stop and take deep breaths. Perform side stretches, as shown on pages 34 and 66. If you are in a race and do not wish to stop, make sure your posture is erect, and take deep abdominal breaths.
Stress fracture Dull ache accompanied by tenderness and swelling; pain returns even after resting for a few days	Persistent shin splints are often a sign of stress fractures. If you suspect a stress fracture, consult a doctor.

Choosing Shoes

The most important piece of equipment for either walking or running is a good pair of shoes. Shoe manufacturers produce a wide selection of walking and running shoes, some of which are represented on the right.

Shoes designed for runners, such as the pair shown at the bottom of the opposite page, generally have thick cushions. When selecting a running shoe, however, you must balance the benefits of cushioning with the shoe's flexibility — its ability to bend easily. Generally, the greater the cushioning and the thicker the shoe, the less flexible it will be. Taller, heavier individuals should look for shoes with greater cushioning; shorter, lighter people should find more flexible shoes.

Walking shoes, such as the pair shown on the right, below, require less cushioning than running shoes. When buying either walking or running shoes, look for heel counters or other stability features that control excessive pronation, or leaning inwards towards the ankles. The shoes should also have leather or leather and mesh uppers, be flexible enough to bend easily at the ball of the foot, and have enough space for you to wiggle your toes comfortably.

If you intend to purchase shoes for hiking, orienteering or walking across rugged terrain, be sure they provide adequate ankle support, such as the pair on the right, above. If you engage in a variety of fitness activities and do not wish to purchase shoes for each application, look for cross-trainers, like those at the top of the opposite page, which combine characteristics of many types of shoes, including cushioning and heel support for walking and jogging, and ankle support and added stability for weightlifting and other activities.

Equipment

In addition to a good pair of shoes, walkers and runners can benefit from additional items such as those shown on the left. Many exercise walkers, for instance, enhance the benefits of walking by carrying hand weights such as those shown on the opposite page, below centre. Many fitness enthusiasts and practically all competitive walkers and runners wear digital wrist-watches called chronographs. As well as displaying the time, a chronograph *(opposite, below right)* can function as a stopwatch for timing yourself.

Hikers who spend a whole day, or perhaps several days, on the trail must depend on a good backpack to carry supplies, and frame packs, such as the one shown opposite, take the weight off the shoulders and dis-tribute it to the buttocks, hips and thighs. Day hikers, who may carry only a plastic water bottle and a sandwich or piece of fruit, may pre-fer a bum pack *(left, below)*, which is a belt with a pouch attached to the back so that it is light and snug.

If you hike in unfamiliar territory, you will also need a topographical map and protractor compass. Topo-graphical maps *(left)* show clearly geographical features, trails and elevations; the protractor compass *(left, below)*, which has a housing that turns on a clear plastic rec-tangular base plate, allows you to align your map to magnetic north to find your way in the wilderness. (See pages 54-59 for tips on how to use a map and a compass.)

CHAPTER TWO

Walking for Fitness

*Techniques to make walking an
effective aerobic conditioner*

At first glance, walking may not
seem like exercise; after all, virtually everybody does it. Many exercise physiologists, however, contend that it is an ideal activity for
anyone who wants to get into shape. Walking is the safest and most
convenient form of exercise for most people to engage in when they
begin an exercise programme. And since it is versatile — you can
vary the intensity, the setting and the style of your workouts and you
can race — walking is also appropriate as a long-term exercise, even
for those who are already in good physical condition.

The greatest advantage of walking as a means to fitness is also,
ironically, its biggest drawback — walking is efficient, which means
that it does not require much energy. Therefore, you can walk for long
periods without taxing yourself. At a casual pace, in fact, walking is
about twice as efficient as running: while a runner lifts himself off the
ground, fighting gravity, a walker uses gravity to his advantage. With
each walking stride, you fall forwards from one foot, swinging the

29

other leg ahead while gathering speed and energy. And when your forward leg strikes the ground and you begin to rise up on that leg, the energy is stored and then released when you stride forwards, only to be gathered up and stored once again in the next gait cycle. The biomechanics of walking is similar to an egg rolling on end: you only have to add a tiny push with each roll to keep it moving. This finely tuned system of energy storage and retrieval means that a person walking at approximately 4 km/h recovers 65 to 70 per cent of the energy he expends with each stride.

Researchers have noted that walking efficiency decreases and the energy you expend increases as you quicken your pace. While a runner burns about the same number of calories to run a kilometre, regardless of the speed, the faster a walker covers a kilometre, the more calories he burns. The crossover point of efficiency between walking and running — that is, when the energy cost of walking exceeds that of running — is about 8 to 9 kilometres per hour. In one study, 10 well-conditioned men aged 22 to 39 were asked to walk at a fast pace for 30 minutes. Walking at about 8 kilometres an hour, all were able to achieve and maintain a pace intense enough to reach their target heart rate, proving that walking is actually an excellent form of exercise for young people who are very fit.

This chapter will show you how you can make walking into an effective exercise, whether you want simply to improve your overall cardiovascular conditioning, to lose weight or to derive aerobic benefits from outdoor leisure-time activity such as orienteering or backpacking. There are several different ways to walk for fitness, as the following pages will show, and you can vary your walking workout to suit your mood or your training goals.

If you are beginning a walking programme, you should start by walking briskly or striding at a pace that raises your heart rate to within 65 per cent of your maximum for about 15 minutes (see the chart on page 13). Warm up for five to 10 minutes before starting the walk, and cool down for an equal time afterwards (see pages 34-37 for warm-ups and cool-downs). Be sure to swing your arms vigorously as you walk. Walk on alternate days, gradually increasing your pace and distance until you can walk at a continuous, brisk pace for 20 to 60 minutes. Do not worry if you find it is uncomfortable to walk much faster than this. Many people can still derive an aerobic benefit from walking at a pace of 5.5 to 7 km/h.

You can increase the effort of walking in other ways besides increasing your speed. Carrying hand weights (*see page 43*) boosts the intensity yet allows you to maintain a comfortable pace. If you pump your arms while you carry hand weights, you will get a workout for your upper body as well as your lower body, and you will make your heart work harder. In addition to boosting the cardiovascular benefits of exercise walking, carrying weights while pumping your arms burns more calories than walking without weights. If you are just beginning a walking programme, do not carry hand weights at first. You should be able to walk a nine-minute kilometre before you intensify your workout by carrying weights.

Climbing stairs is another excellent way that you can keep in shape and add to your lifelong fitness routine. If you live or work in a high-rise building, for example, you should make it a habit to walk up and down the stairs instead of taking the lift. Studies of several groups of office employees showed that those who made use of the stairs instead of depending on the lifts improved their fitness levels by 10 to 15 per cent.

You can also condition your body by augmenting weekday exercise walking with more strenuous weekend hikes. Hiking and backpacking are pleasant pastimes that help you maintain your aerobic conditioning and produce other health benefits. One Appalachian Trail hiker in the United States was tested by exercise physiologists before and after his 87-day, 2,735-kilometre trek, during which he carried a backpack weighing from 16 to 23 kilograms. Because he was already in superb condition, his heart rate while hiking usually hovered somewhat below his target heart range, and his aerobic conditioning at the end of the hike was almost identical to his superb prehike level. But blood tests revealed that his HDL cholesterol, the "good" cholesterol that helps protect against arterial plaque, had risen from 54 to 74. This hiker's experience supports the research findings that frequent long-term activity — even if it is not within a formal workout setting or always intense enough to bring the heart to its target rate — can reduce the risk of cardiovascular disease.

You do not have to hike the Appalachian Trail to reap the benefits of backpacking. One study of 44 individuals aged 18 to 23 examined the effects of walking at a speed of 5 km/h with a light backpack. It showed that walking for 30 minutes a day five days a week for three weeks with a load of 3 to 6 kilograms significantly improved aerobic fitness levels. Although backpacking can be a strenuous activity, it is also reasonably safe: fitness enthusiasts should carry loads of 16 kilograms or less. Backpacking one or two days a week can add variety as well as vigour to any walking programme. (See page 53 for tips on hiking and backpacking.)

Orienteering is another walking activity that is becoming increasingly popular. Since an orienteer's goal is to find a cross-country route between two points and then hike across terrain that may be quite rugged, this sport can be as challenging mentally as it is demanding physically. Those experienced in orienteering use a map and compass to help guide them along country roads and paths, and through the woods, fields and mountains. The ability to find your way through the wilderness is itself an admirable skill, and pathfinding can be an excellent addition to your regular fitness routine. By practising a few simple techniques, you can learn orienteering easily and chart your own course. You can also take part in organized orienteering events. (See page 54 for a more complete description of orienteering and a sample cross-country course.)

If you enjoy the thrill of competing, or if you find that it helps you to feel motivated, you may want to try organized race walking. Race walking is the fastest form of walking: a typical race walker can walk as fast as many people can run. Indeed, the winner of the 20-kilometre walk at the 1988 Seoul Olympics averaged a speed of 15 km/h to set an Olympic record.

The race walker's special gait, however, is as different from ordinary walking as walking is from running. While a runner's feet leave the ground to extend his stride, a race walker's stride is increased by rotational, or rolling, movements of the hips. Early race walkers were called wobblies because of their style. Race walkers can achieve speeds that would be impossible for other walkers to attain. Since the crossover of efficiency between walking and running occurs between 8 and 9 km/h, race walking at a faster speed burns more calories than running. Studies show that the body fat compositions and aerobic capacities of competitive race walkers are similar to those of marathon runners.

Race-walking technique is governed by a stringent set of rules designed to keep at least one of the race walker's feet in contact with the ground at all times. In other words, the heel of the lead foot must strike the ground before the toe of the back foot is lifted. This prevents "lifting", or rising up off the ground like a runner and gaining unfair advantage over other race walkers. You can race walk strictly for fitness, or you can train to enter races. Olympic athletes compete in long-distance walks of 20 kilometres and 50 kilometres, but race walkers compete in walks of many shorter distances. Road-racing officials often allow separate entries in the same race for both race walkers and runners. By competing in running events, race walkers frequently derive impish pleasure from finishing ahead of many runners. Already extremely popular in Europe, race walking is now also catching on in the United States: approximately 45,000 race walkers, many of them over the age of 40, are currently registered with the Walkers Club of America.

Walking of any kind can be a social activity to share with friends or family. You can converse while you walk, and you can combine walking with other activities such as sightseeing, visiting or doing errands. And if you like participating in organized activities, there are numerous walking events and groups to join. In addition to walking clubs and large-scale race walks, sponsored charity walks attract thousands of participants annually.

In country and woodland areas all over the United Kingdom, nature trails and hikes of varying length and difficulty are maintained by bodies such as the National Trust and are freely accessible to the public. Many disused railway tracks have been converted into "linear parks" and these, too, are popular for recreational walking.

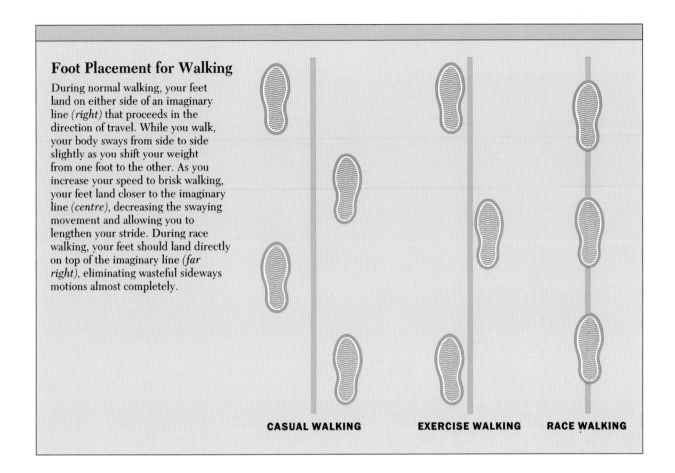

Foot Placement for Walking

During normal walking, your feet land on either side of an imaginary line (*right*) that proceeds in the direction of travel. While you walk, your body sways from side to side slightly as you shift your weight from one foot to the other. As you increase your speed to brisk walking, your feet land closer to the imaginary line (*centre*), decreasing the swaying movement and allowing you to lengthen your stride. During race walking, your feet should land directly on top of the imaginary line (*far right*), eliminating wasteful sideways motions almost completely.

CASUAL WALKING　　**EXERCISE WALKING**　　**RACE WALKING**

Walking enthusiasts often insist that walking is safer than running and many other fitness activities because it is a low-impact sport that results in few injuries. It is true that the impact force of the foot against the ground is quite low in casual walking; however, that impact probably increases substantially during more energetic fitness walking. In addition, while a runner's knee is usually bent on foot strike, allowing the muscles to absorb much of the force of impact, the walker's knee remains straight, and may therefore transmit more of the shock of foot strike to the upper body. Fitness experts suspect that, because of their gait and the speed at whieh they travel, race walkers probably risk the same injuries as runners. (For a description of the types of injuries you can sustain while walking, and how to avoid them, see pages 22-23.)

The clothing you wear while you walk should be comfortable and non-restrictive, such as loose-fitting everyday clothes or a tracksuit. Race walkers usually wear the same outfits as runners. In winter, be sure to wear a woollen cap and gloves to help you retain body heat, which is easily lost at the extremities. If you walk along metalled roads, walk against the traffic and wear bright clothing during the day and reflective patches at night. (For tips on finding the right walking shoes, see pages 24-25.)

Warm-Ups and Stretches/1

Each walking workout should be composed of three segments: warm-up, exercise and cool-down. A warm-up is the preliminary period or practice episode during which you begin to raise your heart rate and metabolic rate to approximately the level of the exercise session. In this way, your heart and muscles will be fully prepared to work for an extended period. A warm-up also prepares you mentally and helps to fine-tune your motor skills for the workout.

Warming up is important, and it is really quite simple to perform. All you have to do is rehearse your activity at a slightly lower intensity than normal. Make it a practice to warm up for five to 10 minutes.

You should also stretch, either after your warm-up or to cool down at the end of your exercise session. Stretching will increase the range of motion in your joints and develop greater muscle flexibility. The routine shown on these two pages and the following two was specifically designed for walkers. Perform each of the stretches for at least 20 seconds. Always be sure to repeat a stretch for one side of your body on the other side as well.

Perform heel raises to stretch and strengthen your calf muscles. Hold on to a stationary object for balance and stand on your toes. Then drop your heels to the ground. Perform at least 20 heel raises.

To stretch your side muscles, grasp your right elbow with your left hand over your head. With your feet apart and knees bent slightly, pull your elbow to the left until you feel a stretch.

Hold on to a stationary object with both hands. Extend your right leg behind you and bend your left knee. Lean forwards until you feel a stretch in your calf and your Achilles tendon.

Stabilize yourself against a stationary object with your left hand. Bend your right knee and grasp your right foot with your right hand. Pull your foot towards your buttocks until you feel a stretch in your thigh.

Sit on the ground and support yourself with your left arm *(above)*. Extend your right leg and place your left foot outside your right knee. Place your right elbow against your left knee and twist to the left.

Lie on your back with your legs extended. Bend your left knee and grasp it with both hands. Lift your head and draw your knee towards your chest until you feel a stretch in your thigh and buttock *(above)*.

Perform windmills to improve the flexibility of your shoulders. Walk at a brisk pace and swing your arms in full circles, alternating sides as if you were performing the backstroke in the water.

To increase hip mobility, cup your hands together and swing them from side to side as you walk briskly. Use a crossover stride so that your left foot is placed on the outside line of your right foot, and vice versa.

Walking Stride/1

Walking at a normal pace is biomechanically very efficient — that is, it does not require much energy. However, as your walking speed increases, your efficiency decreases. The faster you walk, therefore, the faster your heart beats and the more calories you burn. By the time you are walking at a pace of 8 kilometres per hour, you are burning about the same number of calories as if you were running. At speeds higher than this, it is easier and more efficient to run than to walk.

The key to walking efficiently at slow speeds is the biomechanics of the walking gait. As the photographs on these and the following pages show, the proper posture and stride will make your technique efficient.

While walking, you always keep at least one foot in contact with the ground. The foot on the ground supports the body while the raised foot swings forwards. In addition, there is a brief period when both feet are in contact with the ground. At slow speeds, this gait conserves energy. At speeds above 5.5 kilometres per hour, however, it takes an increasing amount of energy to keep both feet on the ground. Therefore, to burn more calories and improve your fitness, you should walk as fast as you comfortably can.

Push off with your right foot and shift your weight to your left leg. During the left-leg support phase, your right leg is free to swing forwards.

At the completion of the right-leg swing phase, strike the ground with your right heel and roll forwards on your left foot. There is a moment of double support.

Shift your weight forwards on your left foot and roll forwards from the right heel. By the time you push off from your toes, your right leg supports your body.

Walking Stride/2

4

5

To get the most from walking, swing your arms forcefully with each stride. At your right heel strike (1), raise your left hand to about chin level. As you begin to shift your weight on to your right foot during the double-support phase (2), swing your left arm down for balance. Both arms are close to your sides (3) during midstance. As you shift your weight forwards from your right foot (4), swing your right arm up to balance your left leg. Then, just before your left heel strike (5), raise your right hand towards chin level.

Increasing the Effort

V irtually anyone can improve his or her fitness by walking regularly. However, a person who is already well conditioned may have to walk uncomfortably fast in order to raise his heart rate to its training zone. (For an explanation of the training zone and how you can determine yours, see page 13.) One study showed that fit young men may have to walk at a pace of 8 kilometres per hour or more to achieve their training heart rates.

Fortunately, walking at high speed is not the only way to get a quality walking workout even if you are very fit. Studies show that you can increase your workload quite significantly by carrying hand weights of 0.5 to 1 kilogram, as long as you swing your arms vigorously and maintain a brisk pace.

While carrying hand weights, be sure to swing them vigorously. When walking up hills, shorten your stride slightly. Do not slacken your pace but keep your head up while you lean into the hill.

Common Walking Mistakes

It is important to maintain good form and posture while you walk. Keeping your head up, your pelvis back and your abdomen tight will improve your respiration and blood circulation.

Yet just because walking is such an automatic activity, many people exhibit poor posture while walking. Poor posture makes you unbalanced and forces the muscles in your head and body to strain to keep your balance. In addition to increasing fatigue, poor walking habits may result in shin splints, lower back pain, and neck and shoulder aches.

These two pages show some common indicators of faulty posture. Monitor yourself from time to time to make sure you are not straining or tightening up, which may indicate fatigue or bad posture.

Slumping can cause neck and lower back pain *(right)*. Tighten your stomach, pull in your buttocks and swing your arms.

Neck and lower back pain can also result from watching your feet *(above)*. Keep your back erect and head up.

If your hands and teeth are clenched, then you are probably tense and stiff *(above)*. Concentrate on relaxing.

Mistakes with Weights

Do not walk with ankle weights *(below, left)*, which may throw off your leg momentum. Avoid bending your elbows when using hand weights *(centre)*; you might hit your head. Do not hold hand weights limply at your sides *(right)*, since that will not improve walking intensity.

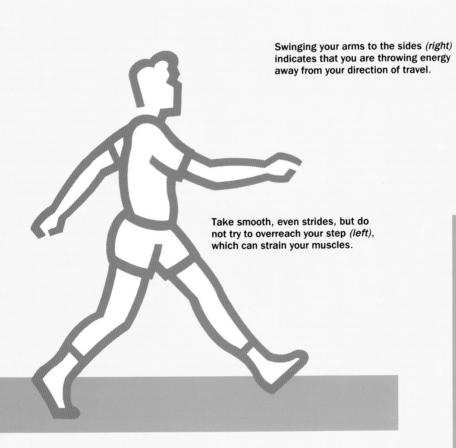

Swinging your arms to the sides *(right)* indicates that you are throwing energy away from your direction of travel.

Take smooth, even strides, but do not try to overreach your step *(left)*, which can strain your muscles.

Race Walking/1

You can walk faster, and thus will burn more calories in a shorter period of time, by race walking than by walking in any other style. The race walker minimizes the double-support phase to a fraction of a second and employs a rolling hip movement to extend the stride length and frequency.

As a competitive activity, race walking is governed by two basic rules to prevent "lifting", or rising off the ground with both feet. First, the advancing foot must make contact with the ground before the rear foot leaves the ground; and second, the supporting leg must be straight in the vertically upright position.

Start race walking slowly, so that you can become accustomed to the gait. Point your toes in the direction of your stride and swing your right leg forwards, reaching with your hip and knee so that you strike the ground with your heel at about a 40-degree angle. Be sure that your leg is straight when your heel hits the ground. Push off with your left foot and keep your right leg straight as your body passes over it to begin the gait cycle again.

Arm movements are also vital in race walking: they add thrust to each stride and assist in giving you balance and momentum. Although race walking may feel like an unnatural movement at first, with practice you should soon feel as if you are gliding lightly or even floating smoothly across the ground.

1

5

Keep your leg straight when your right heel strikes the ground (1). Be sure your leg remains straight as your body assumes a vertically upright position (2). Roll forwards on your right foot and swing your left leg in front of you (3). Push off with the toes of your right foot and extend your left leg (4), making sure that it is straight at heel strike (5). Swing your right leg forwards (6) and roll towards your toes on your left foot (7). Finally, push off on your toes and straighten your right leg for heel strike (8).

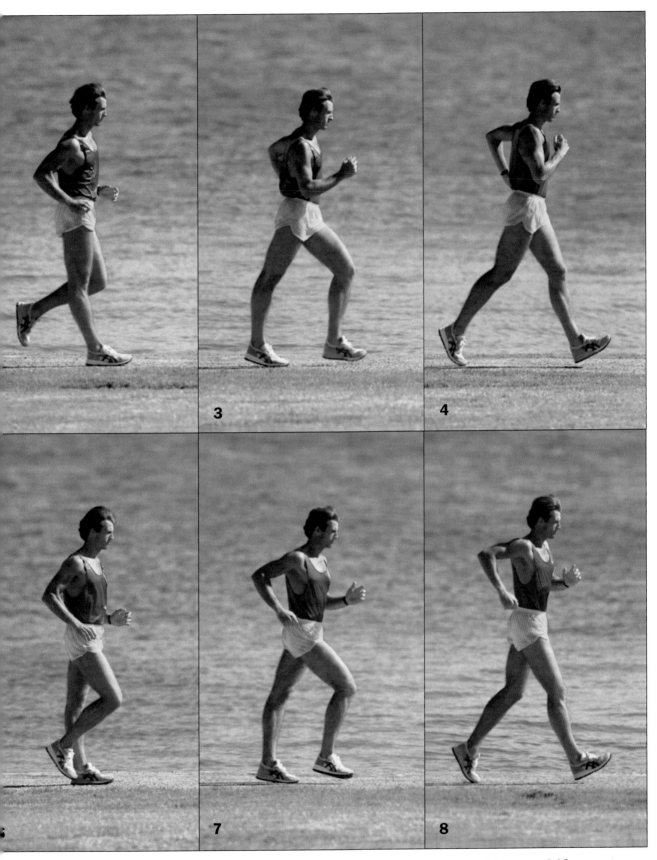

3

4

7

8

47

Race Walking/2

While race walking, one heel must strike the ground before the toes of your other foot lose contact. Plant your feet in a heel-to-toe alignment so that you will be walking along an imaginary line *(left)*.

1

Bend your arms at a 90-degree angle, and keep your hands turned in and cupped slightly. Swing them from just behind your hips to mid-chest level (1). During midstance, your hands should be in front of your hips (2). As you swing your right leg forwards, move your left hand forwards for balance (3). Return to midstance with the right leg supporting your body (4).

Common Race-Walking Mistakes

In the beginning, you will have to pay particular attention to your walking form. And even after you have mastered race walking, and your technique has become second nature, you should review your form periodically to make sure you have not picked up any bad habits. Even top-ranked race walkers can develop sloppy form, especially when they become fatigued.

Do not look down at your feet or watch your hands to see if you are race walking correctly. Instead, try to stay relaxed and loose. If you feel tension in your body, it may be caused by a mistake that is detracting from your performance. It is often a good idea to train with a partner, who can easily spot errors in your form that you do not notice.

Shown on this page are the results of three of the most common race-walking mistakes; on the facing page are three errors in technique that judges look for and that can lead to your disqualification from a race-walking event or competition.

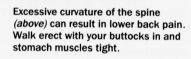

Excessive curvature of the spine (*above*) can result in lower back pain. Walk erect with your buttocks in and stomach muscles tight.

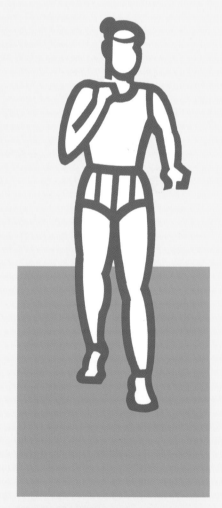

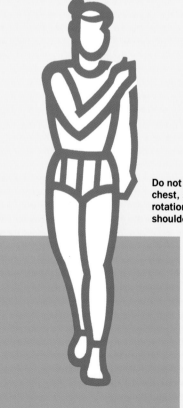

Do not swing your arms across your chest, since this will cause excessive rotational movements of your shoulders and upper body (*left*).

Plant your feet along an imaginary straight line. Otherwise the result is a swaying, side-to-side motion that shortens the distance of each stride (*above*).

Technical Errors

LIFTING Never rise off the ground with both feet *(left)*. Keep your rear foot on the ground until the heel of your leading foot makes contact.

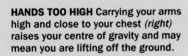

HANDS TOO HIGH Carrying your arms high and close to your chest *(right)* raises your centre of gravity and may mean you are lifting off the ground.

BENT-KNEE FOOT STRIKE A bent knee *(left)* can lead to disqualification in a competitive race-walking event. Make sure your knee is straight when your leading foot hits the ground.

Hiking

In the past 15 years or more, increasing numbers of people have participated in fitness routines such as walking and running and in wilderness pursuits such as camping and canoeing. Hiking combines the elements of both, providing a challenging workout for anyone who loves the outdoors. Although it is not possible for most people to take hikes daily, many walkers find that weekend hikes and backpacking trips provide another dimension to their usual fitness workouts.

In addition to its value as a break in a walker's routine and as an adventure in itself, hiking can be a powerful aerobic conditioner. Few studies have quantified the benefits of hiking, but the experience of hikers themselves makes it clear that hiking can be a strenuous activity demanding a high degree of fitness. One group of hikers and researchers from the Georgia Institute of Technology in the United States, for instance, determined that hiking 240 kilometres in 13 days is the rough equivalent of running 8 kilometres in 40 minutes or less.

Orienteering/1

In addition to its practical value as a means of getting around in the wilderness, orienteering — using a map and compass to find your path between points of land — has special sports and fitness applications. Throughout the United Kingdom and Europe, orienteering clubs regularly hold meets, in which all the entrants are given special topographic-style maps indicating a series of checkpoints, called controls, to find. Hikers must proceed from one control to the next to complete a course. (For tips on selecting the right compass, see page 27.)

On most orienteering maps, the start of a course is drawn as a triangle, the finish as two concentric circles and controls as single circles. Control markers, usually white and red or orange flags, are placed on the course; some may be easy to find, while others may be placed behind a landmark. Lines on the map connecting the control markers show the shortest routes between them, but not necessarily the most desirable ones. These two pages and the following four show a sample orienteering progression from an easily located control in the middle of a field to a marker set behind a tree.

Stand near the control marker and relate your map to the landscape *(right)*. On the map *(opposite, above)*, you are standing at the first control after the triangle in the middle of an open area. The top of the map is north, and you can see the line of trees and heavy vegetation (shown as green patches) to the north and east. Although the most direct route is through the vegetation, a more practical route may be to head north until you hit a trail (line of dashes), where you turn right. Then you can walk southeast to the top of a hill (thin brown contour lines). From there — the attack point — you can plot your route to the second control, which is a tree (small green circle in the centre of the control circle). Having chosen your route, strike out in the northerly direction *(opposite, below)* until you hit the trail.

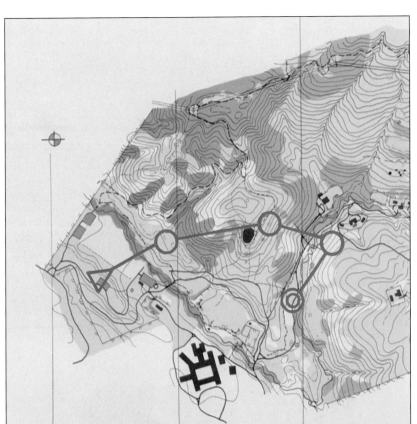

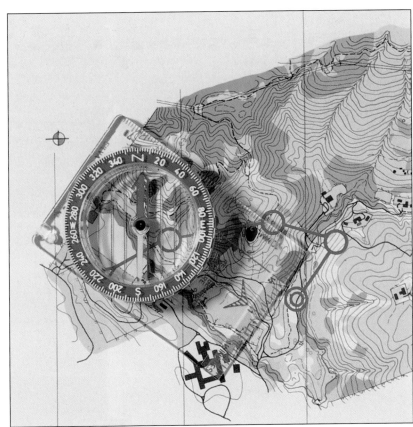

Orienteering/2

Once you have made it to the top of the hill, you have reached your attack point. If you cannot see the control, kneel down and place the map on your thigh *(left)*. Place your compass on top of the map and orient the map so that the red compass needle points to the north end. Then position the base plate of the compass on the map so that one edge connects where you are now, at the top of the hill, and your destination, the next control. Turn the housing of the compass so that the red needle points to both north on the map and north on the housing *(above)*. Since north on orienteering maps is actually magnetic north, to find the next control, merely follow the compass heading — in this case, 120 degrees — shown by the arrow on the compass base.

Orienteering/3

After you have set your bearing, stand up and hold the compass in front of you, with the arrow on the base plate pointing straight ahead *(above)*. Keeping the red compass arrow pointing north, walk in a straight line. If you continue walking in the direction you have plotted, you should soon see the tree indicated on the map. The control marker will be behind it *(right)*.

CHAPTER THREE

Running

*For fun, for fitness and
for competition*

Running is a vigorous conditioner for most of the body's largest and most powerful muscles, especially the heart. Studies have shown repeatedly that running significantly improves cardiovascular fitness for almost everyone, including children and older people. One study has shown that people who began running programmes lowered their blood pressure. And among athletes, the average VO_2max of elite distance runners, according to one survey, is higher than that of every other group of endurance athletes, including competitive cyclists and rowers, elite swimmers and world-class cross-country skiers. Runners in the same survey also showed a lower percentage of overall body fat than any other group.

Running also seems to have a beneficial effect on a person's state of mind: runners commonly report that if they are anxious, angry or depressed, they feel better after a run, and psychological tests confirm that running tends to reduce feelings of stress and anxiety. Running is justly promoted by many doctors and sports-medicine practitioners as both a preventative and a therapeutic activity. No wonder that the

C an running replace psychotherapy? Researchers at San Diego State University gave 12 men and women, aged 23 to 41, a series of initial psychological evaluations. After a one-year programme of running three times a week for 45 minutes, the people were retested. The researchers found, in addition to cardiovascular improvement, that the subjects were more relaxed, assertive and happy-go-lucky, and dealt with abstract concepts more effectively.

President's Council on Physical Fitness and Sports in the United States determined that running, when compared to 13 other popular forms of exercise, was the best activity for cardiovascular fitness, muscle growth, losing weight and relaxation.

In addition to its direct physiological and psychological benefits, running seems to encourage people to eliminate bad habits and adopt a healthier lifestyle. Researchers in the United States surveyed 1,250 randomly selected male and female entrants in the Peachtree Road Race in Atlanta, Georgia. The researchers found that 81 per cent of the men and 75 per cent of the women who smoked cigarettes when they began recreational running had given up the habit by the time they entered this 10-kilometre race. They also determined that weight loss was associated with running: on average, men who were over-weight when they started running lost more than 1 kilogram for every 10 kilometres they ran per week.

The key to many of running's physiological benefits is the bio-mechanical action of the stride. Although the gait is similar for both running and walking, there are significant differences between the two. Speed is determined largely by how fast you can move your legs — your stride rate, style and gait technique — and how far each step reaches — your stride length. When you walk, you always have at least one foot on the ground, and there is a brief period of double support during which both feet are on the ground. Although this makes the walking stride efficient, it slows you down. In contrast, when you run, you literally take off into the air with each stride. The period when you are in the air, called the float phase, accounts for about 30 per cent of your stride. (See the illustration on pages 70-71.)

The great value of running as an aerobic conditioner derives in part from the effort to become airborne required by three groups of the body's most powerful muscles: the calves, the hamstrings and the but-tocks. In addition, the quadriceps muscle along the front of your thigh is required to pull your knee forwards and draw it up to prepare your leg for its next stride cycle. Electromyographic measurements of the electrical activity in the leg muscles show that as you progress from walking to sprinting, your leg muscles become activated for longer periods of time. The hamstrings, for instance, are active during 10 per cent of a walker's stance phase — when the foot is supporting the body — while the same tests indicate that the hamstrings are involved during 80 per cent of a runner's stance phase. Similarly, the calf muscles work during 15 per cent of a walker's stance phase com-pared to 80 per cent of the runner's stance.

Some of the very factors that make running such a vigorous con-ditioner can also cause injuries. For instance, the ground reaction force, which is generated between your foot and the ground, either during push-off or upon impact, can amount to forces of up to 2.8 times your body weight during fast running and perhaps as high as 5.5 times body weight during sprinting. Foot-strike impact can amount to

Problems with Heat and Cold

During hard exercise, muscles can produce 15 to 20 times the amount of heat that they produce at rest. This heat production can raise your body temperature rapidly. Your body can cool itself through the evaporation of sweat. But on hot, humid days or when you are dehydrated and you cannot produce enough sweat, you may not be able to dissipate the heat, causing hyperthermia, a dangerous build-up of internal heat. The early symptoms of this form of heat stress can include headache, nausea, dizziness, clumsiness and excessive sweating or no sweating at all.

Running at a comfortable pace, drinking plenty of fluids and wearing the proper clothing will go a long way towards helping you avoid hyperthermia. On warm days, you should also run in white or brightly coloured clothing made out of cotton or another natural fibre that both reflects the radiant heat of sunlight and allows your body to cool itself through sweating.

Make sure you drink enough fluid before and after you run, and, if you are covering a long distance, during the run. Drink even if you are not thirsty, since you can lose 2 to 3.5 litres of fluid before you notice a thirst, and become dehydrated, which increases the likelihood that you may develop hyperthermia.

Plain water is the best liquid to drink. Have at least one 25-centilitre glass before you begin your run, and at least another 25 centilitres after you have completed it.

Do not run at all if the temperature approaches 32°C and the humidity exceeds 75 per cent. Also, skip your run if the weather is hot and you feel you have a cold coming on.

Too much heat loss from the body, called hypothermia, is not as dangerous to runners as hyperthermia, but it can also present problems. Hypothermia can even occur on only moderately cool days, especially in high altitudes or if conditions are damp and windy.

Early warning signs of hypothermia include shivering, a sense of elation and a feeling of intoxication. On cool and cold days, wear a polypropylene garment near the skin that "wicks" away moisture. Then wear several thin layers of cotton fabric for insulation, with a removable nylon windcheater as an outer layer.

---

a force of 30 Gs. This force causes a vibration that travels up your legs at 320 kilometres an hour like a shock wave to the top of your head.

The human body, however, is able to make a number of biomechanical adjustments to accommodate the effects of this shock wave. When you run, your body increases the flexion of the hips, knees and ankles, thereby lowering its centre of gravity. At heel strike, the runner's flexed knee and ankle allow the contracted muscles that stabilize each joint to act as shock absorbers, which dissipate much of the force of impact. By the time the shock wave hits your hips, the impact has been dissipated to about one-sixth its original strength; when it reaches your head, it is less than one-tenth.

Despite the body's shock-absorbing capabilities, most runners are well aware that they are not immune to injury. In a survey of entrants to a 10-kilometre road race in New York City, researchers found that 46.6 per cent of the respondents had sustained a running injury within the previous two years. Predictably, the researchers found that the injury rate increased with the number of kilometres run per week, the pace and the frequency of competitions entered. The injury rate, surprisingly, was not related to running surfaces, terrain or interval training, which entails spurts of fast running.

Fortunately, the recovery rate among runners is high: 76 per cent of these who consulted a doctor reported a good or excellent recovery from their injuries. Moreover, most running injuries can be prevented, first and foremost by wearing a good pair of running shoes and by not pushing yourself too hard. (For a review of running injuries and how to recover from them, see pages 22-23.)

If you have never run before, or if you are out of shape, begin your training programme by alternating brisk walking with slow jogging for 20 minutes three times a week. As your muscles and tendons become adjusted to the stress, gradually lengthen the time you run and shorten the walking time until you can sustain a run for the full 20 minutes. The guidelines and sample workouts on pages 20-21 show how to develop a programme that is both varied and progressive.

Be sure to warm up properly before each workout and to cool down afterwards. As you build up your stamina, you can pay more attention to your running form, which will increase your efficiency by reducing bouncing motions. The techniques shown on pages 70-77 will make running more enjoyable and also help you to avoid injury.

Ideally, running should be viewed not as a monotonous chore, but as a holiday, a retreat from life's daily demands. But while many people are perfectly happy performing a 20-minute meditative jog several times a week, others do become bored. If you are interested in adding variety and adventure to your running regimen, this chapter will show you various options you can pursue, from training with a partner to entering "fun runs" — races in which winning is not a concern — and various competitive events.

Studies show that runners who enter races and fun runs tend to become long-term fitness enthusiasts. The survey of Peachtree Road Race entrants determined that most of them appeared to be dedicated runners: almost 90 per cent of the men and 80 per cent of the women were still running one year after the race. In addition to the motivation spur that competition provided for these runners, friends also worked as a support group, providing camaraderie.

Although you do not have to compete to be a good runner or to continue on a running programme successfully, many people find that weekend races and fun runs provide motivation on many levels. Running beginners, for instance, may be inspired to train well enough to complete a local 5 or 10-kilometre race. Objectives for more experienced runners may be to improve their time, complete a longer race or perhaps finish before a friend or another runner who has been faster in a previous race.

Once you have entered some races, you may decide to train to improve your time. To be reasonably sure of completing a race, your minimum weekly distance should be at least twice that of the race you plan to run. A weekly base of 30 or more kilometres will not

Pace and Posture

Runners experience slight but significant posture differences as they increase speed, as shown by the two figures on the right, which are silhouettes of an elite middle-distance runner filmed while running on a treadmill. At 10 kilometres per hour — the equivalent of a six-minute-kilometre jogging pace — the runner is more upright, his body has an up-and-down motion and his stride rate is moderate. When he doubles his speed to 20 kilometres per hour — the pace of an elite marathon runner — his body slants forwards and his stride length and rate increase.

As you increase your running speed, therefore, you use new muscles or the same muscles in slightly different ways. Exercise physiologists believe that to prepare for competition, you must train at about the same pace as you plan to race, replicating race conditions as closely as possible. In this way, your muscles can rehearse the movements and postures they will undergo during the competition.

10 km/h

20 km/h

only prepare you to finish the race, but will probably also help you to run faster and more strongly.

In addition to accumulating kilometres to improve your endurance, your strength and speed will also be dramatically enhanced by running hills repeatedly, by including running timed interval workouts on the track, and by performing a technique called "fartlek", or "speed play". Developed by the coach of the 1948 Swedish Olympic Team, fartlek workouts are usually run with at least one other person and often consist of alternating easy running with untimed sprints over varied terrain. While on a fartlek run, you can play games such as tag, toss a ball back and forth, or challenge your partner to short races. Since it helps boost performance, fartlek training is used by many runners.

By making up games to play while you run, by giving yourself attainable goals and by entering fun runs and weekend races, you can make running an enjoyable activity rather than just a solitary ordeal. Instead of providing merely a rigid exercise prescription, this chapter will also give you some tips on entering races, which can be social events as well as self-motivating competitions.

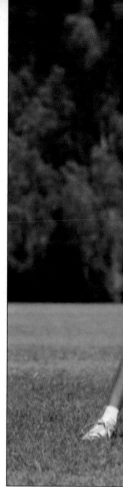

Spread your feet and place your hands on your hips. Keeping your back straight, bend to the right, then forwards, to the left and backwards.

Stretches/1

Runners frequently tend to rush through their preliminary stretches, or do not stretch at all. But stretching after you have warmed up is vital to your physical training: it increases joint range of motion and muscle suppleness, and thus helps prevent injury.

Flexibility will help you to avoid injury in three ways: first, supple muscles and tendons are less prone to tears and strains than stiff ones; second, flexible muscles and good joint range of motion reduce the chance of sprains; and third, muscle elasticity places less strain on adjacent joints. A runner with tight hamstrings, for instance, is not only at a higher risk for leg muscle and tendon injuries, but may also injure his knees, lower back and hips.

Be sure to warm up your muscles before you stretch. You can stretch before or after a run, as long as you warm up by running on the spot or taking a short jog first. Warming up increases the blood flow to muscles and helps make them loose.

Do not bounce when you stretch; this "ballistic" stretching may actually injure the muscles you are trying to protect. Always perform relaxed and deliberate stretches. Never push yourself to the point of pain, though the final stage of a stretch should be slightly uncomfortable.

Hold each of these stretches for 20 seconds, then relax. You may repeat the stretch if you wish. If you perform a stretch on one side of your body, be sure to repeat the stretch on the opposite side.

Hold your arms out to the sides, parallel to the ground with your feet spread, then bend at the waist and reach your right hand towards your left toes.

Place your hands against a fence. Bend your right knee and extend your left leg, easing your heel towards the ground until you feel a stretch in your calf.

Squat on the ground, supporting yourself with your hands. Extend your left leg, drawing your right leg to your chest.

Stretches/2

Lie on your back, bend your left knee, grasp it with both hands and draw it towards your chest *(top)*. Then extend your arms to the sides to stabilize your upper body, and cross your left leg over your right. Keeping both shoulders on the ground, extend your left foot towards your right hand *(above)*.

Sit on the ground, extend your left leg and draw your right foot to your left thigh. With both hands, slowly reach towards your extended foot.

Sit on the ground and draw the soles of both feet together. Hold your feet and move your knees towards the ground as far as you can to stretch your adductors.

Running
Stride/1

Many runners mistakenly think of running as a bouncing motion rather than a continuous movement, and you may notice that the heads of inexperienced runners often bounce. In fact, one researcher has calculated that an inexperienced marathon runner may bounce so much that he or she runs the equivalent of up to 1.5 kilometres vertically.

In a truly efficient stride, such as the one shown here and on the following two pages, the runner's head barely moves up and down during any portion of the stride.

When you run, try to think of propelling yourself forwards. If you do not bounce, your body will have a lower centre of gravity, thus giving you a longer and more powerful drive. In addition, your knees and ankles will be more flexed, helping them to absorb road shock.

You can also use your arms to improve your running technique. Do not hold them limply at your sides when you run; pump them as if you were punching to improve your speed and power. The faster your arms move, the faster your legs move. Never let your hands swing away from your hips or across the middle of your chest. Allow your elbows to stick out slightly in order to counterbalance the rotation your feet make with each stride.

PUSH-OFF Extend your rear leg to propel yourself forwards, not upwards. Meanwhile, lift your front knee so that it pulls forwards while the rear knee is extended. The calf muscles of your rear leg draw you up on your toes to push you forwards.

FLOAT After the push-off phase, your body becomes airborne. The float phase extends your stride so that you can move faster when you run than when you walk. Be sure to look ahead; looking down will shorten your stride.

TOUCHDOWN If you run efficiently, you should touch down on the outside rear of your foot, rather than on the heel, which allows greater weight distribution. You should feel more of a quick slap on the ground than a hard impact.

1

2

Running Stride/2

To maintain a relaxed stride, keep your shoulders back,
chest out and buttocks in (1). During the float phase, do
not overextend your stride; allow your legs to extend
naturally (2). As your hands swing back and forth, they
should occasionally brush lightly against your shorts (3).
If you feel tension in your shoulders, hands or jaw,
remind yourself to relax; unclench your jaw, loosen your
hands and drop your shoulders (4).

4

Sprinting

For fun, for variety or during competition, you may want to increase your speed. Maintaining good form, though, becomes all the more important when you sprint. Since sprinting is essentially an anaerobic activity that requires more strength than endurance, you can quickly become fatigued. When this occurs, you rapidly lose your form, efficiency and speed.

The key to fast running is to train often and pay attention to your form. Do not worry about your pace at first. Simply run as fast as you can for short distances — 100 metres, for instance — without sacrificing your form. Once you become accustomed to running fast in good form, perform timed intervals on a track to increase your stamina and overall sprinting speed *(pages 92-93)*.

When sprinting, think of your feet as spokes of a wheel and keep them moving quickly. Use your arms to punch the air *(below)*. Your hands should never become fists or flop about; keep them relaxed and turn your palms in slightly *(below, left)*. Maintain an erect posture and move forwards on your feet so that you touch down close to your toes *(opposite, right)*. Do not bounce, but slap the ground with your foot *(opposite, left)*.

75

Learn to "fall" uphill by leaning forwards; use a short stride and push from your toes. Pretend you are using your arms to pull yourself up a rope *(opposite)*. Do not sprint down a hill; stay relaxed and allow yourself to "fall" so that you can catch your breath, yet still maintain speed. Lean forwards and land on the balls of your feet. Instead of pumping your arms, keep them low to maintain balance *(left)*.

Hills

Running uphill may be taxing, but nothing can help you to build leg power better or condition you faster than hill work. In addition, it sharpens your mental toughness and builds the physical stamina required to race.

The technique of running uphill is fairly simple, although problems that you have running on a flat surface are magnified when you go up a slope. Practise your technique by running hard up a 500 to 1,000-metre hill with a 10 to 15 per cent gradient. Do not stop at the crest; continue to run hard over the top. Then keep running downhill, quickly but staying relaxed, to regain your breath. Once you are back on level ground, turn round to climb the hill again. Training in this manner is called running repeat hills. You may run repeat hills once or twice a week, but never on consecutive days, to give your body time to recover.

Although running down a hill takes about two-thirds as much energy as running up the same hill, downhill runs are more jarring to your body and are more likely to cause injury. Also, downhill runs are more likely to leave you with sore muscles a day or two later, because your muscles will be unaccustomed to resisting the forward momentum. This soreness will diminish with continued training, however, as your muscles become more relaxed when running downhill. If possible, train on grass at first; you can become accustomed to the slope while keeping the impact to a minimum.

Common Running Mistakes

Running technique can be idiosyncratic and still be highly effective. And you would never be disqualified from a race for bad running form. However, many runners — and beginners in particular — make wasteful movements that detract from their performance and contribute to fatigue and the risk of injury.

If you watch a top-ranked long-distance runner during a marathon, you may think that he is running at a relaxed and leisurely pace. However, if you clock the pace of the leading contenders, you may find that they are running three-minute kilometres. The key to this apparently effortless movement is running efficiency: there is not a single wasted movement, and no sign of strain. Running three-minute kilometres for about 42 kilometres is certainly not a leisurely pace; it only appears so because most elite runners maintain their form effectively.

You can improve your pace by eliminating wasteful movements that can drain your energy. These two pages illustrate the six most common mistakes that are made by runners and suggest ways to correct them.

OVERSTRIDING *(right)* Do not lunge forwards with your feet, but allow a natural stride. Focus on a short, fast arm swing.

LOSING DOWNHILL CONTROL *(left)* This may cause injury or the fear of it. Drop your hands, shorten your stride and run with a more erect posture.

WIDE ARM SWINGS *(left)* Keep the palms of your hands turned in and slightly up to help keep your elbows near your sides.

HUNCHED SHOULDERS *(right)* This indicates tension. Shake your shoulders and hands to loosen up and relax.

LANDING ON YOUR HEELS *(left)* Shorten your stride and increase your lean slightly, landing towards the balls of your feet.

RUNNING ON YOUR TOES *(left)* This indicates that you are bouncing too high. Lean forwards and lengthen your stride.

Conditioning Routines

Some runners can enhance their performance with strengthening exercises that exaggerate running form. Two such techniques are called bounding and prancing. When you practise bounding, you leap in the air and pump your arms powerfully to create as much lift as possible. This is an exhausting exercise, but one that will strengthen your shoulders, thighs and calves.

Prancing is not quite so tiring, but requires good balance and strong abdominal muscles to perform well. Although this is an exercise to improve your running, it is actually a walk, since you always have at least one foot on the ground. To do it, rise up on your toes and walk by lifting your knees high. Land only on your toes. This exercise teaches you to keep your knees high and your legs and arms moving quickly. It also helps you to move up on to your toes when you are sprinting.

Use these strengthening exercises to break up your regular running routine. Start off by bounding and prancing on a 25-metre stretch of grass or earth. When you become stronger, you can progress to 100 metres. Perform these drills no more than twice a week, and never on consecutive days.

To bound, leap as high as you can with each stride *(top, left)*. Pump your arms powerfully to give yourself as much lift as possible *(top, centre)*, and extend your legs fully, landing on your forefoot *(top, right)*.

To prance, rise up on your toes and lift the opposite knee until your thigh is parallel to the ground *(bottom, left)*. Pause briefly and then step down, again rising up on your toes *(bottom, centre)*. Continue walking in this manner, making sure your heels do not touch the ground *(bottom, right)*.

Partner Running/1

Although many distance runners enjoy the solitude of their pursuit, others prefer company on their runs, finding that both time and distance pass more quickly with a friend. Indeed, sports psychologists at the University of North Carolina and Louisiana State University found that at light and moderate levels of intensity, exercisers perceived their exertion levels to be easier when they exercised with a partner.

In addition to the psychological benefits of running with a friend, a partner can help improve your motivation through friendly competition and give pointers on your technique.

Running with a partner can make fartlek running more enjoyable. Fartlek is a loosely structured form of training during which you alternately run fast or easily, depending on your mood or the terrain. While running with a partner, for instance, you can challenge each other to short races, play tag or invent other games. Fartlek runs ease your sense of exertion and also increase your feelings of exhilaration and fun.

Most people find training partners entirely by chance; for example, you may notice someone running in a local park who appears to be at your level, or a neighbour may suggest that you work out together. You can also seek training partners actively by appearing at running clubs or races and talking to other runners. However you find your partner, you can ensure the greatest benefit by choosing someone whose ability is closely matched to your own — and by following the tips presented on the next six pages.

Partner Running/2

To minimize the level of exertion you perceive and still maintain a high-quality workout, do not race your partner; take turns at leading. Drop a step or two behind your partner and "ride" her shoulder *(far left)*. If you look at a spot on her shoulder and match her stride, you can be "pulled" along. Change places periodically by surging round your partner *(centre)* and take the lead so that she can ride your shoulder *(left)*.

Partner Running/3

You can intensify the leading and riding technique shown on pages 84 and 85 by placing a series of cones, rocks or other markers at varying intervals along a course or round a field. Ride your partner's shoulder as he runs the course at a fast pace *(left)*. As you approach one of the cones, surge ahead so that you pass your partner when you reach the cone *(above, left)*. Do not race your partner, but keep your pace strong as he rides your shoulder. Your partner should begin to surge ahead as you approach the next cone *(above, right)*.

Partner Running/4

Play games with your partner occasionally to increase your enjoyment, prevent boredom and help you look forward to your next run. For instance, bring a ball with you and throw it back and forth while you run *(below)*.

A game of tag is not only fun; it will also help improve your ability to surge and sustain a sprint, either to pass someone in a race or to hold off another runner who wants to pass you *(above)*.

The Long Run

A weekly long run forms the backbone of any endurance-running programme; it is important for strengthening your heart and improving oxygen delivery to your working muscles. Long runs also teach your body not to rely exclusively on the glycogen stored in your muscles as an energy source: they require you to use body fat for energy, so that you not only spare some glycogen, but also burn off body fat as you run.

Long runs can also give you a psychological advantage for shorter races: if you complete a run of 16 kilometres once a week in addition to your usual shorter runs, you will find that completing an 8-kilometre race seems relatively easy.

Many runners perform a long run about once a week. In runs that may last an hour or two, many prefer to run in groups to help the time and the distance pass more quickly. Running clubs often sponsor after-work or weekend group runs of 20 to 30 kilometres and runners frequently look forward to these as social gatherings as well as endurance training. If the group is large, runners may break up into units, each one proceeding at its own pace.

Your long run should not be more than about one-third of your total weekly distance. Plan your run in advance so that you can drink water along the route, especially in hot weather. Some runners carry water bottles with them; others prefer to carry money so that they can stop to buy bottled water along the way.

Intervals

Interval training is the antithesis of the long run. Instead of endurance training over varied terrain, intervals require that you run timed sprints over measured distances with a short period for recovery between sprints. Usually, the recovery period consists of getting your breath while you jog.

Intervals allow you to train at a higher intensity than you would normally encounter in competition. Distance runners typically perform interval training twice a week. Not only do intervals help increase your speed, but they also give you the mental stamina needed in a race.

Most tracks are about 400 metres. Running on a track can put you in a mood to race, and many runners find that they run intervals too quickly. As a result, they become exhausted early in the workout, losing the benefit of interval training. Do not run each interval at an all-out pace; run each one a little faster than your normal fast pace. If you run 400-metre intervals, for example, run each at a slightly faster pace than you would run 1,500 metres.

A beginner's workout may comprise six to eight 400-metre intervals with a 200-metre recovery jog between them. Try to run each 400 metres in 1:40-1:43 time. You can also run three or four 800-metre intervals with a 200-metre recovery.

As your strength and speed improve, you can cut your recovery time and increase the number of intervals. See the chart on pages 106-107 for a typical weekly training schedule that incorporates intervals.

Road Racing

Running beginners most often get their first taste of road racing at distances between 5 kilometres and 10 kilometres. The 10-kilometre, or 10-K, race has long been a staple of long-distance road running. Although marathons steal the bulk of media attention, these shorter events are far more popular among runners. A large part of the appeal in entering 5 to 10-K races is that many people routinely train about that distance for them.

Training for and running in 5 to 10-K races are likely to increase your aerobic capacity. Studies show that oxygen consumption of top athletes during a 5-K race is about 98 per cent of maximum, and in a 10-K race about 90 per cent. If you improve your oxygen consumption by running these races, your performance is likely to improve.

Whatever distance you run for your first race, you should not be concerned about your finishing time. Concentrate on enjoying yourself and completing the race. Perhaps when you enter your second race you can better your time. In that case, wear a watch and keep track of kilometre markers if the course has them. Then you can gauge your pace, the distance you have covered and the distance remaining, so that you can expend your energy accordingly. If the course does not have markers, use your usual training pace as a guide to determine how far you have run after a specific elapsed time. (Realize that you will probably run faster when you race.)

The Marathon

No other running experience can equal that of competing in a marathon, the gruelling 42.2-kilometre (26.2-mile) endurance race. Runners often aspire to a marathon as either the goal or the high point of their training.

Long considered to be the limit of human endurance, the marathon taxes the strength and stamina of even the most highly trained athlete. To be minimally in shape to complete a marathon, you should run at least 65 kilometres a week for six weeks, and have run at least two 30-kilometre training runs. In addition, you should run several shorter races, of from 3 to 25 or 30 kilometres, to gain experience before you attempt to run a marathon.

The week before the race, taper off your training and jog lightly the day before the marathon. On the morning of the race, have a light, bland breakfast of dry toast and fruit juice. Arrive at the start at least an hour early to check in, stretch and warm up. Be sure to bring petroleum jelly to rub on the inside of your thighs, feet and other places where friction may cause chafing or blisters. Pack extra shoelaces, another pair of running shoes, safety pins for fastening your race number to your jersey and dry clothing to wear after the race. Tie your shoelaces with a double knot before you begin the race.

The eight pages that follow give you guidelines and tips on actually running various portions of a race; you can apply this advice to running a marathon as well as to competing in shorter-distance events.

Starting the Race

The first step in a running event is deciding where your starting position should be. If you stand at the front, it is likely that faster runners will push you aside. If you start at the rear, you will spend a lot of energy just running round other competitors.

In crowded races, unless you are an elite athlete and deserve to stand in the front line, it is best to say at a spot in the middle of the field. Then you can pick up your pace during the race when the congestion thins out, rather than risk tripping or bumping into someone at the start.

Do not begin the race with a sprint; aim for a strong, steady pace. By the 2.5-kilometre point in a 10-kilometre race, you should have found a pace that will carry you through most of the distance. In a marathon, it may take you as long as 10 kilometres to find your pace.

Maintaining Your Pace

Theoretically, the perfect race will consist of even splits — meaning that each kilometre is run at exactly the same pace — and a fast finish. Few races follow a predetermined plan, however. Instead, you will probably find tactical reasons to speed up or slow down for various portions of the race, according to how you feel and what sort of conditions, including other runners, are present.

Once you have found your pace *(see page 99)*, you may want to run in a small group. Settle in with a group that wants to finish the race in about the same time as you do. You may find yourself matching other runners' strides step for step, and you may even feel yourself pulled along by them as you run.

Another benefit of running in a group is that you can use the others to build your own confidence. Listen to their breathing and talk to them briefly to gauge how they feel. One runner may dominate the group and set the pace. Ride this leader's shoulder, if you feel you can keep up, or stay just a half step behind. When the leader surges, follow him; you can use his speed to spur your own. Or, if you are capable, leave the pack of runners behind and enter a faster group, or run by yourself, aware that the pack is following you.

Water Stops

Virtually all races of 10 or more kilometres will feature water stops. While a 10-kilometre race may offer water only at the halfway point and the finish, large urban marathons frequently boast water tables every few kilometres. It is important during a race, particularly in races longer than 10 kilometres, to drink water whenever possible. On a hot day, you should drink even if you are not thirsty; otherwise, you will very probably become dehydrated.

Drinking on the run is an art that takes practice to perfect. Take the water cup in one hand and squeeze it gently to form a spout. Then raise it to your lips and take short sips.

If you cannot drink and run at the same time, stop for a moment and drink. Some runners also take a cup of water and pour it over their heads. The water on your head may feel great for a few seconds, but it will not cool you down. Studies show that even water sprays are not sufficient to reduce your core body temperature while you run. Only drinking cool water at regular intervals will prevent dehydration.

The Finish

If you want to make a strong finish, do not wait until you see the finishing line to kick into a sprint. If you do, the chances are that you will be outkicked.

When other runners are tiring towards the end of the race, use your arms to pump and pick up your pace. Increase your pace at the 7-kilometre point of a 10-kilometre race. In a marathon, pick up your pace with 1.5 kilometres to go, so that your time will be faster and you will have a better chance of breaking away.

Once you cross the finishing line, jog slowly or walk to cool down. If the weather is the least bit cool, be sure to keep moving and put on warm clothing as soon as possible. Drink water or fruit juice. Although some runners enjoy drinking beer after races, it is better to avoid alcohol until you are completely re-hydrated, since alcohol is a diuretic that can increase dehydration.

Part of finishing every race is the recovery period, which may last for days or even weeks after a particularly strenuous race. Runners often become injured by returning to their normal workouts too soon after a race. Take it easy for the first day or two, and exercise moderately if you feel particularly sore and stiff. Jog, cycle, swim or walk briskly until your legs recover from the race, and stretch frequently.

Run half your usual distance for the first week after a race, then increase the kilometres gradually during the second week. If you enter races as part of your regular training, you may be able to race two or three times a month. However, do not attempt to run two marathons in less than three months.

Training to Race

For your first race or two, you may only be interested in enjoying the experience and in completing the distance. During additional races, however, you may want to improve your time.

If you are just starting out, begin your training slowly, as outlined on pages 20-21. Comprehensive studies by Soviet researchers have proved that no single system of training — intervals, hill work, fartlek or endurance running — is on its own the most effective way to train. The best approach is to utilize all of these techniques. The schedule shown on the right outlines a general plan that includes both distance running and interval work.

To adopt the greatest variety of training techniques, most schedules utilize the principle of alternating hard and easy workouts. If you run hard intervals on Tuesday, for instance, run an easy 12 to 15 kilometres on Wednesday. Likewise, if you run hills or fartlek one day, perform a long, steady run the next.

In addition to running alternate hard and easy days, many competitive runners also employ double workouts on some of their hard days. A double workout incorporates two training sessions; for example, a long, slow run in the morning and track intervals in the early evening.

Keep in mind that every runner is different. The schedule on the right is only an example and not necessarily one that you should follow strictly. For best results, try to consult a coach or an experienced competitor to help you devise an optimal schedule that fits your goals.

MONDAY

TUESDAY

WEDNESDAY

THURSDAY

FRIDAY

SATURDAY

SUNDAY

	WEEK *1*	WEEK *2*	WEEK *3*	WEEK *4*
	15 km	15 km	15 km	15 km
A.M. **P.M.**	12 km 15 x 400 m	6 x 1.5 km 12 km	12 km 15 x 400 m	7 x 1.5 km 12 km
	12 km	15 km	12 km	15 km
A.M. **P.M.**	10 km 10 x 800 m	4 x 2.5 km 10 km	10 km 10 x 800 m	5 x 2.5 km 10 km
	10 km	5 km	10 km	10 km
	12 km	10 km	12 km	5 km
	OFF	OFF	OFF	RACE

CHAPTER FOUR

Strength Conditioning

A programme for walkers and runners

Even if you walk or run 8 kilometres a day or more, you are probably not doing all you can to develop your overall fitness. Walking and running are excellent cardiovascular conditioners — and certainly develop the powerful muscles of your thighs, calves and buttocks — but they do not exercise your upper body. Traditionally, competitive walkers and runners believe that nothing conditions their bodies better than simply more walking and running. However, inspired by the success of elite athletes who have incorporated weight training into their programmes, more and more competitors and fitness enthusiasts alike are discovering the benefits of upper body workouts. By developing your muscle strength and joint stability, weight training can increase your endurance and speed, help prevent injuries and improve your posture.

The upper body does far more than just provide the lower body with a stable hinge from which the legs can swing back and forth. Studies show that the arms and shoulders not only help balance the body in motion, but also contribute as much as 10 per cent to a runner's vertical lift. This additional lift gives the runner more "flight" time, so that his foot stride is extended considerably and his running speed is increased. The more powerfully the arms pump, therefore, the faster will be the running speed.

Strong arms and shoulders are also important for walking, but for different reasons. Because at least one foot is always in contact with the ground when you walk, your arms do not contribute to vertical lift. In casual walking, the arms and shoulders act simply to counterbalance the swinging motion of the legs. However, as your walking speed increases, so does the contribution of your upper body. When you race walk, your shoulder and arm swings transmit torque and power to the hips, contributing up to 50 per cent of the propulsive force of your stride. Arm and shoulder movement also helps keep you "on track", that is, moving forwards along a straight line without unnecessary side-to-side weight shifts.

To test the importance of your arms and shoulders to your walking speed, try walking as fast as you can while you keep your shoulders rigid and your arms at your sides. Then race walk, pumping your arms and shoulders powerfully: you will notice that not only is it easier to walk with your arms and shoulders moving, but your stride length, cadence and walking speed also increase.

A good walker or runner must utilize the dynamic contribution that the upper body can make to endurance, speed and stride. To do so, you should develop your upper body to complement your lower body training. According to exercise physiologists, the more closely your strength conditioning reflects the activity for which you are training, the more effective it will be. This is called the principle of specificity. Following this concept, many of the exercise routines in this chapter mimic body postures and movements which you use frequently in your normal daily walking and running workouts.

Moreover, for maximum effectiveness, your weight-training programme should target the same types of muscle fibres that your regular workout exercises. Sprinters, for instance, are most concerned with strength and speed. Physiologists know that top-ranked sprinters have highly developed fast-twitch muscle fibres, which are recruited for sudden bursts of power. Since working out with heavy weights selectively trains the fast-twitch muscle fibres, many sprinters incorporate weight-training exercises in their routines.

The muscles of elite marathon runners and race walkers, in contrast, contain predominantly slow-twitch fibres, which are used for endurance exercise. Lifting lighter weights repeatedly will develop slow-twitch muscle fibres. If you are a fitness walker or a distance runner, and you want to improve your performance, you should not be working out with heavy weights. Instead, train with weights somewhat below your maximum capacity, repeating each exercise 20 to 40 times. By performing many repetitions, or reps, which will closely

Working Out with Weights

◆ To warm up before you lift weights, walk briskly, jog on the spot or skip for five to 10 minutes. Warming up will improve your muscle and joint range of motion and help to reduce your chance of sustaining an injury.

◆ Train with free weights no more than three times a week, and always allow at least one day of rest in between workouts. This will prevent overtraining, which can result in muscle fatigue, soreness and injury.

◆ Keep track of your progress on a chart or in a journal. Be sure to indicate the exercises you perform, the weights you lift and the number of repetitions in each set. When you note that you can lift a particular weight for more than your usual number of reps for two or three consecutive workout sessions, graduate to a heavier weight.

◆ With experience, you should be able to judge how much to increase the effort in order to gear your weight training to your walking or running. If you are running strictly for distance, for instance, you may wish to increase your reps to 40 or more. If you are running to increase your speed, or if you are increasing your hill work, cut back on the number of reps and increase the amount of weight you lift. To work on both strength and endurance, weight train in sets of 10 reps. Perform 10 reps, pause, then perform two more sets of 10 reps. You should lift enough weight so that by the tenth rep of the final set, you are too exhausted to perform another rep.

parallel your fitness-walking or endurance-running programmes, you will develop your slow-twitch fibres — with some crossover benefit to your fast-twitch fibres.

Train your muscles by using the technique of progressive resistance. Since your muscles adapt to the stress you place on them, they will grow stronger only if you increase the demand progressively. You can do this by increasing the number of reps to improve muscle endurance, or by increasing the amount of weight to develop muscle strength. In this way, you can fine-tune your weight-training programme to complement your regular workouts (box, above).

If you are a distance runner, you need not worry that weight training will develop muscle bulk so much that it interferes with efficient running: the slow-twitch fibres targeted by using lighter weight and many reps do not increase in size substantially. Upper body muscles maintain moderate mass even though their endurance capacity increases.

You can perform your workout at home or in a gym. However, you may find that exercising at home is the most convenient and least expensive alternative. All you need to start are a set of dumbbells, an exercise bench and a mat. You can lift weights in your usual exercise attire, but be sure to wear enough clothing to keep warm; cold muscles are less flexible and tend to become injured more easily than warm muscles. Warm up for five to 10 minutes before you begin to lift weights; cool down for the same amount of time afterwards.

Upper Body Routine/1

To build your upper body, perform an exercise routine with dumbbells, an exercise bench and a floor mat. This chapter provides a complete conditioning regimen to strengthen all the major muscles in your upper body. Like most routines, it starts with the larger muscles of the upper back and chest, and then progresses to the smaller muscles. This order helps prevent fatigue. As this routine is designed specifically for walkers and runners, it incorporates unilateral swinging motions of the upper arms and shoulders whenever possible, which mimic walking and running arm motions and positions.

Unless otherwise indicated, perform one set of 20 to 30 repetitions for each exercise, or follow the guidelines in the box on page 111. Lift weights that are heavy enough to exhaust your muscles temporarily at the end of each set, but not so heavy that you are unable to complete the set. If a routine shows an exercise for one side of your body, be sure to repeat the same exercise for the other side. Perform these exercises two or three times a week, with at least one rest day between workouts.

Perform pullovers to strengthen your upper back. Lie face up on an exercise bench. Hold a dumbbell in your left hand, and bring it over and behind your head, until you feel a stretch in your chest *(left, top)*. Keep your elbow bent slightly and lift the weight over your chest *(left, centre)*. Lower the dumbbell to your abdomen *(left)* and return to the starting position.

Perform bent-over rows to strengthen your back and upper arms. Bend over an exercise bench and support yourself with your left hand. Hold a dumbbell in your right hand *(above)*. Lift the dumbbell straight up to your chest *(above, right)* and then lower it to the starting position.

To strengthen your lower back muscles, lie face down on an exercise mat with your arms at your sides. Raise your chest and shoulders off the floor, keeping your pelvis in place *(left)*. Return slowly to the starting position.

113

Upper Body Routine/2

Perform a dumbbell bench press to work your chest, shoulders and triceps. Lie face up on an exercise bench and hold two dumbbells just a little wider than shoulder-width apart *(right)*. Press both the dumbbells straight up simultaneously without locking your elbows *(far right)*. Return to the starting position.

A bent-arm fly is similar to the bench press. Without locking your elbows, raise two dumbbells over your chest *(right)*. Lower your arms to your sides until you feel a stretch in your chest *(far right)*. Return to the starting position.

114

Upper Body
Routine/3

Perform lateral arm raises to strengthen your shoulders. Stand erect with your knees bent slightly, while holding the dumbbells at your sides. Raise the dumbbells laterally until your arms are parallel to the floor *(below)*. Return to the starting position to complete one repetition.

Perform single arm raises to further strengthen your shoulders. Hold the dumbbells at your sides and stand with your knees bent slightly. Keeping your elbow bent, raise your right arm in front of you until the dumbbell is at shoulder height *(above)*. Lower your right arm; raise and lower your left arm in the same manner *(above, right)*.

You can also perform shoulder shrugs for your trapezius muscles. Stand erect and hold the dumbbells at your sides. Lift your shoulders straight up *(right)*; then return to the starting position.

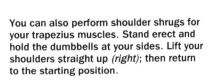

Upper Body Routine/4

**Perform arm curls to strengthen your biceps muscles. Stand
erect with your knees bent slightly, and hold the dumbbells
at your sides. Bend your right elbow and raise the dumbbell
to chest level** *(above)*. **Return to the starting position, and
repeat for your left biceps** *(above, right)*.

To perform triceps extensions, bend over an exercise bench and support yourself with your right hand. Hold a dumbbell in your left hand, but keep your upper arm and elbow next to your body *(left)*. Keeping your upper arm in the same position, extend your lower arm *(left, below)*. Return to the starting position.

Upper Body Routine/5

Perform bent-knee curls to strengthen your abdominals. Lie
face up on a mat with your hands behind your head and your
lower legs supported on an exercise bench *(above)*. Tighten
your abdominals and raise your head and shoulders and upper
back off the floor *(opposite)*. Return to the starting position.

To increase the intensity of the bent-knee curl shown above, hold a light weight disc behind your head and perform the same exercise *(right)*. Avoid pulling against the back of your head or your neck.

121

Upper Body Routine/6

Perform lateral side bends to strengthen and stretch your sides and the muscles between your ribs. Stand erect with your knees bent slightly and your right hand behind your head *(above, left)*, holding a dumbbell with your left hand. Bend to the left, allowing the weight of the dumbbell to pull your left arm and shoulder towards the floor *(above)*. Return to the starting position.

Perform crossover sit-ups for your obliques, or side muscles. Lie on your back, place your hands behind your head and cross your right foot over your left knee *(left, above)*. Keeping your right elbow on the floor, raise your left shoulder and upper back *(left)*. Return to the starting position.

CHAPTER FIVE

The Right Diet

*Quality nutrients — and convenient
recipes — to enhance endurance*

he most important fuel for walking
and running — as for all activity requiring endurance — is food rich
in complex carbohydrates. This nutrient, which is derived from
cereals, grains, fruits and vegetables, supplies at least 50 per cent of
the energy you need for moderate activity. When you are very active,
this percentage increases significantly: a person who runs at 75 per
cent of his VO_2max, for example, derives nearly all of his energy
from stored carbohydrates. In fact, studies have shown repeatedly that
athletes on a high-carbohydrate diet have three times the endurance of
athletes on a diet high in fat. Although fat can also be a source of
energy, food that is rich in fat can be metabolized easily only in
the presence of carbohydrates. A very small amount of energy comes
from protein; its primary function is to build and repair cells and
tissues. And carbohydrates are also necessary for the regulation of
protein metabolism in the body.

All carbohydrates are composed of sugars. Simple sugars include
fructose and glucose from fruits and vegetables; sucrose, refined from

125

sugar cane or sugar beets; and lactose, or milk sugar. These sugars are broken down to their simplest forms, absorbed in the small intestine during digestion and converted by the body into glucose, the form of sugar found in the bloodstream. Your body uses some of this sugar to maintain a constant level in the blood, since your cells need to take sugar from the bloodstream for energy. A small amount of the excess is stored in the liver and muscles in the form of glycogen, which can be reconverted to usable glucose for the cells, while the rest goes to form body fat.

Complex carbohydrates, as long chains of sugars are known, are derived from plant starches and from the fibre that forms the outer shell of grains and other plant foods. Ultimately, the starches are broken down into glucose — just as the simple sugars are. The body can store only a small amount of these sugars as glycogen — to a maximum of 1,500 calories, or about 350 grams — and any excess calories in complex carbohydrates will be stored as body fat. Recent research has suggested that calories derived from fat are more likely to become body fat than those derived from complex carbohydrates, but these findings are still considered controversial.

Body fat is the primary way that animals store energy; each kilogram of fat contains 9,250 calories, of which 7,700 can be used for fuel. In comparison, plants store energy as carbohydrates, and each kilogram of carbohydrates contains 3,750 calories, of which a much smaller percentage can be used for fuel than calories stored as fat. (Carbohydrates also form fibre in plants. When this fibre is part of your food, it is generally not metabolized, but passes through the body more or less unchanged.) While fat is a much more efficient energy-storage medium, it is metabolized at a significantly slower rate than carbohydrates. Endurance athletes depend on carbohydrates as an important exercise fuel for this reason. And since carbohydrates cannot be stored in large amounts, exercisers must replace what they use by eating foods rich in carbohydrates.

Foods high in complex carbohydrates not only fuel endurance, but are also often nutritionally rich. Many of them contain protein, and they are almost always high in vitamins and minerals, which makes them a better choice than foods high in fat or simple sugars. In recent years, most nutritionists have come to believe that consuming 55 to 60 per cent of your total calories mostly in the form of complex carbohydrates is the healthiest way to eat. You should derive a maximum of 30 per cent of your calories from fats, and approximately 11 per cent of your calories from protein sources. (The introductory notes that accompany the recipes in this chapter point out some of the nutritional bonuses of a diet that contains plentiful amounts of the high-carbohydrate foods that are recommended.)

Studies have shown that eating complex carbohydrates soon after exercise is an effective way to replace muscle glycogen. Some researchers believe that endurance athletes can also benefit from a diet

The Basic Guidelines

For a moderately active adult, Britain's National Advisory Committee on Nutrition Education recommends a diet that is low in fat, high in carbohydrates and moderate in protein. The committee's proposals for the long term suggest that no more than 30 per cent of your calories come from fat, that around 11 per cent come from protein and hence that 55 to 60 per cent come from carbohydrates. A gram of fat equals nine calories, while a gram of protein or carbohydrate equals four calories; therefore, if you eat 2,100 calories a day, you should consume approximately 70 grams of fat, 310 grams of carbohydrate and 60 grams of protein daily. If you follow a low-fat/high-carbohydrate diet, your chance of developing heart disease, cancer and other life-threatening diseases may be considerably reduced.

◆ The nutrition charts that accompany each of the low-fat/high-carbohydrate recipes in this book include the number of calories per serving, the number of grams of fat, carbohydrate and protein in a serving, and the percentage of calories derived from each of these nutrients. In addition, the charts provide the amount of calcium, iron and sodium per serving.

◆ Calcium deficiency may be associated with periodontal diseases — which attack the mouth's bones and tissues, including the gums — in both men and women, and with osteoporosis, or bone shrinking and weakening, in elderly women. The deficiency may also contribute to high blood pressure. The daily allowance for calcium recommended by the United Kingdom Department of Health and Social Security (DHSS) is 500 milligrams a day for men and women. Pregnant and lactating women are advised to consume 1,200 milligrams daily.

◆ Although one way you can reduce your fat intake is to cut your consumption of red meat, you should make sure that you get your necessary iron from other sources. The DHSS suggests a minimum of 10 milligrams of iron per day for men and 12 milligrams for women between the ages of 18 and 54.

◆ High sodium intake is associated with high blood pressure in susceptible people. Most adults should restrict sodium intake to about 2,000 milligrams a day, according to the World Health Organization. One way to keep sodium consumption in check is not to add table salt to food.

technique called carbohydrate loading, which entails eating considerably more than the recommended 55 per cent of carbohydrates before a competition. But this regimen has been shown to be effective only, if at all, for exercise that lasts for a minimum of 90 minutes, when stores of muscle glycogen are depleted.

This chapter presents recipes that generally supply more than 55 per cent of calories in the form of carbohydrates. They do not comprise a balanced diet by themselves, but help to boost your carbohydrate intake. The pulses, rice, pasta, fruits and vegetables included here are all low in fat. If you are embarking on a walking or running programme, or if you compete in either activity, you will benefit from including these recipes in your diet. And since, by weight, carbohydrates have the same number of calories as proteins but fewer than half the calories of fats, a high-carbohydrate/low-fat diet makes weight control relatively easy to accomplish.

Currant Muffins

Breakfast

CURRANT MUFFINS

A cinnamon-raisin Danish pastry contains about 40 per cent more fat and 30 per cent less carbohydrates than one of these muffins.

CALORIES per muffin	170
80% Carbohydrate	35 g
10% Protein	4 g
10% Fat	2 g
CALCIUM	77 mg
IRON	2 mg
SODIUM	242 mg

175 g (6 oz) plain flour
150 g (5 oz) yellow cornmeal
3 tablespoons sugar
2 teaspoons baking powder
¾ teaspoon bicarbonate of soda
¼ teaspoon salt

30 g (1 oz) margarine, melted and
  cooled
125 g (4 oz) currants
1 egg
25 cl (8 fl oz) skimmed milk

Preheat the oven to 200°C (400°F or Mark 6). Line 12 muffin tin cups with paper liners; set aside. In a medium-sized bowl, stir together the flour, cornmeal, sugar, baking powder, bicarbonate of soda and salt. Rub in the margarine, then stir in the currants. Make a well in the centre; set aside. Beat the egg in a small bowl, then stir in the milk. Pour the egg mixture into the dry ingredients and stir until just combined. Divide the batter among the muffin tins (they will be nearly full) and bake for 25 minutes, or until the muffins are golden-brown on top and a toothpick inserted in the centre of a muffin comes out clean and dry.

Makes 12 muffins

BLUEBERRY COBBLER

*The carbohydrates in the fruit and crust will keep your energy level
high, while the minimal amount of fat in the crust keeps this breakfast
from "weighing you down" all morning long.*

CALORIES per serving	180
71% Carbohydrate	32 g
5% Protein	2 g
24% Fat	5 g
CALCIUM	73 mg
IRON	1 mg
SODIUM	208 mg

**300 g (10 oz) fresh or frozen
  blueberries**
3 tablespoons pure maple syrup
75 g (2½ oz) plain flour
¾ teaspoon baking powder

½ teaspoon ground cinnamon
⅛ teaspoon salt
20 g (¾ oz) margarine, melted
1 tablespoon skimmed milk
1 teaspoon grated lemon rind

Preheat the oven to 200°C (400°F or Mark 6). Very lightly oil a shallow
22 cm (9 inch) pie dish; set aside. If using fresh berries, wash, dry, stem and
pick them over. Combine the berries and maple syrup in a small saucepan
and cook over medium heat, stirring occasionally, for 5 minutes, or until the
berries are very soft; remove the pan from the heat and set aside.

Combine the flour, baking powder, cinnamon and salt in a medium-sized
bowl and stir to combine. Stir in the margarine, milk and lemon rind, and mix
until a soft dough forms. Turn the dough on to a lightly floured surface and roll
it out with a floured rolling pin to a 22 cm (9 inch) round about 3 mm (⅛ inch)
thick. Stir the berry mixture, pour it into the pie dish and lay the crust on top.
Bake the cobbler for 25 minutes. Leave it to cool for 5 minutes, then cut it into
quarters and serve warm.   Makes 4 servings

FRENCH TOAST WITH RASPBERRY-ORANGE SAUCE

*The glucose in whole grains is released more slowly than that in refined
products, making wholemeal bread a superior fuel for the athlete.*

17.5 cl (6 fl oz) skimmed milk
4 tablespoons orange juice
**1½ teaspoons grated
  orange rind**
2 eggs
½ teaspoon ground cinnamon
¼ teaspoon grated nutmeg

8 slices wholemeal bread
**350 g (12 oz) fresh or frozen
  raspberries**
2 tablespoons brown sugar
20 g (¾ oz) margarine
8 orange segments for garnish

In a medium-sized bowl, whisk together the milk, orange juice and rind, eggs,
cinnamon and nutmeg. Lay the bread slices in a large baking tin and pour the
milk mixture over them, turning the bread once to coat it with the mixture; set
aside for 20 minutes. Tilt the pan occasionally to enable the bread to absorb
all the liquid. Meanwhile, combine the raspberries and sugar in a food processor or blender and process until puréed. Strain the purée through a sieve,
then transfer it to a small jug and set aside.

Melt half the margarine in a large non-stick frying pan over medium-high
heat. Add four slices of bread and cook for 4 minutes on each side, or until
golden-brown. Melt the remaining margarine in the pan and cook the remaining bread in the same fashion. Divide the French toast among four plates, top
each serving with sauce and garnish with orange segments.

Makes 4 servings

CALORIES per serving	320
62% Carbohydrate	52 g
14% Protein	12 g
24% Fat	9 g
CALCIUM	176 mg
IRON	3 mg
SODIUM	353 mg

RAISIN BUTTERMILK WAFFLES WITH STRAWBERRY PURÉE

CALORIES per serving	245
65% Carbohydrate	40 g
11% Protein	7 g
24% Fat	7 g
CALCIUM	113 mg
IRON	2 mg
SODIUM	218 mg

In addition to providing 40 grams of carbohydrates, these fruit-topped waffles supply good amounts of vitamin C, calcium and potassium, all important nutrients for athletes. Vitamin C assists in the conservation of glycogen, the body's main muscle fuel, thereby enhancing endurance. Calcium acts in concert with exercise such as walking and running to build strong, dense bones. Potassium helps regulate the body's water balance and is involved in energy release within the muscles; insufficient potassium can cause muscle weakness and cramping during exercise.

200 g (7 oz) fresh strawberries	15 cl (¼ pint) buttermilk
1½ teaspoons icing sugar, or less to taste	150 g (5 oz) plain flour
1 egg, separated	1½ teaspoons caster sugar
20 g (¾ oz) margarine, melted and cooled	¾ teaspoon baking powder
	⅛ teaspoon bicarbonate of soda
	4 tablespoons raisins

Wash, dry and hull the strawberries. For the strawberry purée, combine half the berries with ¾ teaspoon of icing sugar in a food processor or blender and process for about 1 minute, or until smoothly puréed. Slice the remaining berries and set them aside separately.

Preheat the oven to 95°C (200°F or Mark ¼). Preheat a non-stick waffle iron. (If your waffle iron does not have a non-stick surface, oil it lightly before preheating it. Do not re-oil the hot waffle iron.) In a small bowl, whisk together the egg yolk, margarine and buttermilk until blended; set aside. In a large bowl, combine the flour, caster sugar, baking powder and bicarbonate of soda and stir until well mixed; set aside. In a medium-sized bowl, whisk the egg white until it is stiff but not dry. Add the buttermilk mixture to the dry ingredients and stir until blended, then stir in the raisins. Using a rubber spatula, gently fold in the egg white.

Pour about 15 cl (¼ pint) of batter into the centre of the waffle iron, spread it evenly with the rubber spatula, and cook for 5 minutes, or according to the manufacturer's instructions, until the waffle is golden. Place it on a heatproof platter, cover it loosely with foil and place it in the oven to keep warm. Make another waffle in the same fashion. Divide each large waffle into four, place two small waffles on each of four plates and top each serving with one quarter of the purée. Arrange the sliced strawberries on top, sprinkle the waffles with the remaining icing sugar and serve. Makes 4 servings

Bean and Tuna Salad

Lunch

BEAN AND TUNA SALAD

The beans in this salad provide more than four grams of protein — and virtually no fat — as well as slowly released glucose for lasting energy.

CALORIES per serving	310
61% Carbohydrate	47 g
17% Protein	13 g
22% Fat	8 g
CALCIUM	107 mg
IRON	4 mg
SODIUM	384 mg

6 tablespoons lemon juice
2 tablespoons olive oil
2 tablespoons chopped parsley
1 teaspoon chopped fresh
   rosemary, or ½ teaspoon
   dried rosemary
¼ teaspoon black pepper
Pinch of salt
250 g (8 oz) carrots, peeled
   and diced

150 g (5 oz) spring onions,
   coarsely chopped
125 g (4 oz) celery, diced
45 g (1½ oz) water-packed
   canned white tuna
200 g (7 oz) cooked white beans,
   rinsed under cold water
   and drained if canned
12 large round lettuce leaves
175 g (6 oz) French bread

For the dressing, whisk together in a small bowl the lemon juice, olive oil, parsley, rosemary, black pepper and salt. In a large bowl, toss together the carrots, spring onions and celery. Drain the tuna. Add the beans and tuna to the salad, pour the dressing over it and toss gently. Let the salad stand at room temperature for at least 30 minutes, or refrigerate it for at least 2 hours. Meanwhile, wash and dry the lettuce. To serve, line four plates with lettuce leaves and spoon the tuna salad on top; serve the bread with the salad.

Makes 4 servings

STUFFED MUSHROOM BAKE

Most packet casserole-sauce mixes are very high in sodium. This dish is made with a fresh tomato sauce to which only a touch of salt and a sprinkling of Parmesan cheese are added.

1 tablespoon olive oil	1 teaspoon each chopped fresh
8 very large fresh mushrooms,	thyme and rosemary, or ½
stalks removed and chopped	teaspoon each dried
850 g (1¾ lb) onions, peeled and	¼ teaspoon black pepper
coarsely chopped	90 g (3 oz) brown rice, cooked
2 tablespoons low-sodium	500 g (1 lb) fresh tomatoes, diced
chicken stock	4 tablespoons chopped fresh
½ teaspoon salt	basil, or 1 tablespoon dried
3 garlic cloves, crushed	2 tablespoons grated Parmesan

CALORIES per serving	210
66% Carbohydrate	36 g
12% Protein	7 g
22% Fat	5 g
CALCIUM	102 mg
IRON	3 mg
SODIUM	336 mg

Preheat the oven to 180°C (350°F or Mark 4). Heat the oil in a large frying pan over medium heat. Add the mushroom caps, hollow side up, and sauté for 3 minutes. Transfer the caps to a plate and set aside. Add the mushroom stalks, half of the onions, 1 tablespoon of stock, ¼ teaspoon of salt, the garlic, thyme, rosemary and pepper to the pan. Cook, stirring, for 5 minutes, then add the rice and cook for 3 minutes more. Transfer to a bowl.

For the tomato sauce, heat the remaining stock in the pan, add the remaining onions and cook, stirring, for 5 minutes. Add the tomatoes, basil and remaining salt, and cook, stirring, for 5 minutes more.

Spoon half of the tomato sauce into the bottom of a 20 cm (8 inch) square baking tin and spoon about half of the rice mixture on top. Lay the mushroom caps, hollow side up, on the rice and spoon the remaining rice mixture over and around them. Pour the remaining tomato sauce over the mushrooms and sprinkle them with Parmesan. Cover the tin with foil and bake for 15 minutes, or until heated through.   Makes 4 servings

CHICKEN-NOODLE SOUP WITH VEGETABLES

The body requires more of the B vitamins thiamine and riboflavin during strenuous exercise. These vitamins, supplied by pasta, play a crucial role in the body's production of energy from dietary carbohydrates and fats.

CALORIES per serving	195
62% Carbohydrate	31 g
12% Protein	6 g
26% Fat	6 g
CALCIUM	52 mg
IRON	3 mg
SODIUM	234 mg

2 tablespoons olive oil	175 g (6 oz) linguine or other fine
325 g (11 oz) carrots, peeled	noodles
and diced	20 g (¾ oz) parsley, chopped
150 g (5 oz) spring onions,	2 tablespoons chopped fresh dill,
chopped	or 2 teaspoons dried
1 sweet green pepper, diced	½ teaspoon salt
75 cl (1¼ pints) low-sodium	½ teaspoon black pepper
chicken stock	

Heat the oil in a medium-sized frying pan over medium heat. Add the carrots, spring onions and green pepper, and sauté for 4 minutes, or until the carrots are softened. Add the stock and 25 cl (8 fl oz) of water and bring the mixture to a simmer. Break the linguine into 5 cm (2 inch) lengths and stir them into the soup. When the soup returns to a simmer, stir in the parsley, dill, salt and pepper, and cook for another 10 minutes, or until the linguine are *al dente*. Ladle the soup into six bowls and serve immediately.   Makes 6 servings

MINESTRONE

Hot soup is welcome after a cold-weather walk or run: it warms the body while replenishing depleted fluids and carbohydrates. This home-made soup contains only about half the sodium of canned minestrone and about five times as much potassium.

CALORIES per serving	305
71% Carbohydrate	57 g
20% Protein	16 g
9% Fat	3 g
CALCIUM	108 mg
IRON	6 mg
SODIUM	471 mg

90 cl (1½ pints) low-sodium
  chicken stock
550 g (1 lb 2 oz) potatoes, peeled
  and diced
400 g (14 oz) fresh tomatoes, diced
200 g (7 oz) courgettes, diced
200 g (7 oz) cooked kidney beans,
  rinsed and drained if canned

125 g (4 oz) carrots, peeled
  and diced
30 g (1 oz) parsley, chopped
2 tablespoons tomato paste
1 garlic clove, crushed
½ teaspoon salt
¼ teaspoon pepper
2 tablespoons grated Parmesan

Bring the stock to the boil in a large pan over medium-high heat. Add the potatoes, reduce the heat to medium and cook for 15 minutes, or until barely tender. Add the rest of the ingredients except the Parmesan, and return the mixture to a simmer. Cook for 30 minutes, or until the vegetables are very tender. Ladle into four bowls and sprinkle with Parmesan.   Makes 4 servings

BAKED POTATO WITH HERBED YOGURT SAUCE

Potatoes, virtually fat-free and high in complex carbohydrates, are an ideal food for walkers and runners. They are a very good source of vitamin C and potassium, especially when they are baked and the skins are eaten. The herbed yogurt and cottage cheese topping is a satisfying substitute for soured cream or butter.

CALORIES per serving	205
80% Carbohydrate	43 g
17% Protein	9 g
3% Fat	1 g
CALCIUM	119 mg
IRON	4 mg
SODIUM	231 mg

4 large baking potatoes, about
  250 g (8 oz) each
12.5 cl (4 fl oz) plain low-fat
  yogurt
60 g (2 oz) low-fat cottage cheese
4 tablespoons chopped parsley

2 tablespoons finely chopped
  fresh chives
150 g (5 oz) spring onions,
  chopped
¼ teaspoon salt
¼ teaspoon white pepper

Preheat the oven to 180°C (350°F or Mark 4). Wash and dry the potatoes, then bake them for about 1¼ hours, or until tender when pierced with a sharp knife. Meanwhile, for the sauce, combine the remaining ingredients in a medium-sized bowl, and stir until well blended; set aside. When the potatoes are done, cut them open and scoop about half of the flesh into a bowl. Mash with a fork, then add to the sauce and stir until blended. Divide this mixture among the potatoes, and serve.   Makes 4 servings

Dinner

CALORIES per serving	355
68% Carbohydrate	61 g
15% Protein	13 g
17% Fat	7 g
CALCIUM	97 mg
IRON	5 mg
SODIUM	509 mg

CHINESE BEEF SAUTÉ

The iron in beef is better absorbed by the body than that in vegetables.
Iron helps make haemoglobin, which carries oxygen to the muscles.

175 g (6 oz) long-grain white rice
250 g (8 oz) carrots, thinly sliced
1 tablespoon vegetable oil
125 g (4 oz) topside or braising
  steak, cut into thin strips
1 each sweet red and green
  peppers, cut into thin strips
150 g (5 oz) spring onions,
  chopped
3 garlic cloves, crushed

150 g (5 oz) Chinese cabbage,
  shredded
250 g (8 oz) fresh mushrooms,
  thinly sliced
16 water chestnuts, thinly sliced
3 tablespoons low-sodium soy
  sauce
2 tablespoons rice wine vinegar
1 teaspoon sugar
¼ teaspoon hot red pepper flakes

Bring 50 cl (16 fl oz) of water to the boil in a medium-sized pan over medium-high heat and stir in the rice. Cover the pan, reduce the heat to medium low

Chinese Beef Sauté

and simmer for 15 minutes, or until the rice is tender and the water is absorbed. Meanwhile, bring a large saucepan of water to the boil. Blanch the carrots in the boiling water for 3 minutes, or until tender but still crisp; drain, cool under cold running water and set aside to drain thoroughly. When the rice is cooked, remove the pan from the heat and set aside.

Heat the oil in a large, non-stick frying pan or wok over medium-high heat. Add the beef, and sauté for 3 to 4 minutes, or until browned. Using a slotted spoon, transfer the beef to a small bowl and set aside. Add the peppers, spring onions and garlic to the pan and cook, stirring occasionally, for 5 minutes. Add the carrots, cabbage, mushrooms, and water chestnuts, increase the heat to high, and cook, stirring frequently, for 5 minutes. Meanwhile, in a small bowl stir together the soy sauce, vinegar, sugar and pepper flakes. Add this mixture, the rice and the beef to the pan, and cook, stirring constantly, for 4 to 5 minutes, or until the ingredients are heated through. Divide the mixture among four plates and serve.   Makes 4 servings

PESTO PIZZA

This pizza offers a substantial amount of calcium without excessive fat because it is topped with a comparatively low-fat cheese. The vegetables, flour and even the herbs provide some calcium, too. This mineral helps maintain proper muscle function in the heart, lungs and extremities.

1¼ teaspoons dried yeast	20 g (¾ oz) fresh basil,
Pinch of sugar	chopped
100 g (3½ oz) plain flour	2 tablespoons grated Parmesan
30 g (1 oz) wholemeal flour	250 g (8 oz) red onions
1 tablespoon olive oil	250 g (8 oz) aubergine
¼ teaspoon plus a pinch of salt	350 g (12 oz) tomatoes
5 large garlic cloves	60 g (2 oz) low-fat mozzarella
1 tablespoon chopped walnuts	cheese, grated

CALORIES per serving	260
56% Carbohydrate	38 g
16% Protein	11 g
28% Fat	8 g
CALCIUM	193 mg
IRON	2 mg
SODIUM	294 mg

In a medium-sized bowl, stir together the yeast, sugar and 6 tablespoons of warm water (40-45°C/105-115°F); set aside for 5 minutes. Add the plain flour, 3 tablespoons of wholemeal flour, the oil and ¼ teaspoon of salt, and mix well. Flour the work surface with 1½ teaspoons of wholemeal flour and knead the dough for 5 minutes. Rinse and dry the bowl. Place the dough in the bowl, cover with a damp tea towel and set aside to rise in a draught-free place for 40 minutes, or until doubled in bulk. Meanwhile, for the pesto, bring a small saucepan of water to the boil. Add the garlic cloves, and cook for 5 minutes; peel them and place in a food processor or blender. Add the walnuts, basil, Parmesan, the remaining salt and 4 tablespoons of water. Process the mixture for 1 minute, or until thick and smooth; set aside. Peel and trim the onions. Wash and trim the aubergine and tomatoes. Cut the onions, aubergine and tomatoes into thin slices; set aside.

Preheat the oven to 240°C (475°F or Mark 9). Knock back the dough. Flour the work surface and a rolling pin with the remaining wholemeal flour and roll out the dough to a 30 cm (12 inch) round. Transfer it to a baking sheet and crimp the edges to form a rim. Spread the pesto evenly over the crust and top it with the vegetables. Sprinkle with mozzarella and bake for 15 minutes, or until the cheese is bubbly.   Makes 4 servings

CALORIES per serving	405
74% Carbohydrate	76 g
15% Protein	15 g
11% Fat	5 g
CALCIUM	81 mg
IRON	5 mg
SODIUM	326 mg

ORIENTAL PASTA WITH MANGE-TOUT AND PEPPERS

Raw vegetables provide the most vitamins and minerals, but when cooked quickly, by blanching or steaming, they retain most of their nutrients. The broccoli and mange-tout provide calcium, while the sweet peppers are an excellent source of vitamin C. In fact, a serving of this pasta dish supplies more than twice the recommended daily requirement of this vitamin.

250 g (8 oz) mange-tout
1 each sweet red and yellow
  peppers
150 g (5 oz) broccoli florets
350 g (12 oz) fine noodles
4 tablespoons low-sodium
  chicken stock

1 tablespoon vegetable oil
2 tablespoons low-sodium
  soy sauce
2 tablespoons lemon juice
2 teaspoons finely chopped
  fresh ginger
1 garlic clove, crushed

Bring a medium-sized saucepan of water to the boil. Meanwhile, wash and trim the mange-tout. Wash, seed and coarsely dice the peppers; set aside. Blanch the mange-tout in the boiling water for 30 seconds, or until they turn bright green. Reserving the boiling water, transfer the mange-tout to a colander, cool them under cold running water and set them aside to drain. Blanch the broccoli florets in the boiling water for 3 minutes, or until tender but still crisp; cool them and set them aside to drain thoroughly.

Bring a large pan of water to the boil. Cook the noodles in the boiling water for 10 minutes, or according to the packet directions, until *al dente*. Meanwhile, cut the mange-tout in half diagonally. For the dressing, combine the remaining ingredients in a small bowl; set aside. Drain the noodles and transfer them to a large serving bowl. Add the vegetables and dressing, and toss to combine. Serve immediately.   Makes 4 servings

CALORIES per serving	290
74% Carbohydrate	56 g
16% Protein	12 g
10% Fat	4 g
CALCIUM	176 mg
IRON	4 mg
SODIUM	415 mg

STUFFED AUBERGINE

If weight control is one of the goals of your exercise programme, remember that high-fibre foods help to keep you feeling full. This dish provides six grams of dietary fibre per serving.

2 small aubergines (about
  750 g/1½ lb total weight)
250 g (8 oz) onions
3 garlic cloves
4 tomatoes (about 400 g/14 oz
  total weight)
1 large sweet red pepper
4 tablespoons low-sodium
  chicken stock

20 g (¾ oz) parsley, chopped
½ teaspoon dried thyme
½ teaspoon dried oregano
½ teaspoon black pepper
12.5 cl (4 fl oz) skimmed milk
1 tablespoon chopped walnuts
2 tablespoons grated Parmesan
2 tablespoons wheat germ
250 g (8 oz) French bread

Preheat the oven to 180°C (350°F or Mark 4). Wash and trim the aubergines and halve them lengthwise. Place the halves cut side down on a foil-lined baking sheet and bake for 30 minutes, or until tender. Meanwhile, peel and coarsely chop the onions and garlic. Wash, core and coarsely dice the tomatoes and sweet pepper; set aside.

Leaving the oven at 180°C (350°F or Mark 4), remove the aubergines and set them aside to cool slightly. Meanwhile, for the stuffing, heat the stock in a large frying pan over medium heat. Add the onions and garlic, and cook, stirring occasionally, for 3 minutes, until softened. Add the sweet pepper, and cook, stirring, for 3 to 4 minutes. Add the tomatoes, parsley, thyme, oregano and ¼ teaspoon of black pepper, and cook, stirring frequently, for 5 minutes. When the aubergines are cool enough to handle, carefully scoop out and reserve the flesh, leaving a shell about 1 cm (½ inch) thick. Coarsely chop the reserved aubergine flesh, add it to the frying pan, and cook for another 3 minutes. Remove the pan from the heat and set aside.

For the topping, combine the milk, walnuts, Parmesan, wheat germ and remaining black pepper in a small bowl, and stir well. Place the aubergine shells in a baking dish and fill them with the stuffing. Spoon the topping mixture over the stuffing, spreading it evenly. Cover the dish with foil and bake for 30 minutes. Five minutes before the aubergines are done, wrap the bread in foil and place it in the oven to warm. Cut the bread into slices and serve it with the stuffed aubergines.　　　　　　　　　　　　　　　　　Makes 4 servings

INDIAN CHICKEN WITH POTATOES AND CARROTS

Strong bones are a must for runners, and vitamin A is necessary for proper growth and development of the skeleton. Sweet potatoes are an excellent source of beta carotene, the precursor of vitamin A. It is converted to vitamin A only as the body requires it, making it a safer source than vitamin A supplements.

CALORIES per serving	305
64% Carbohydrate	50 g
17% Protein	13 g
19% Fat	7 g
CALCIUM	129 mg
IRON	3 mg
SODIUM	350 mg

125 g (4 oz) skinned and boned
　chicken breast
12.5 cl (4 fl oz) plain low-fat
　yogurt
1 tablespoon lemon juice
1 teaspoon curry powder
½ teaspoon ground cumin
⅛ teaspoon cayenne pepper
½ teaspoon salt

½ teaspoon black pepper
500 g (1 lb) potatoes
1 orange-fleshed sweet potato
250 g (8 oz) carrots
250 g (8 oz) onions
5 garlic cloves
1½ tablespoons olive oil
1½ tablespoons chopped
　fresh coriander

Cut the chicken into four pieces. In a glass bowl, stir together the yogurt, lemon juice, curry powder, cumin, cayenne pepper, ¼ teaspoon of salt and ¼ teaspoon of black pepper. Add the chicken to this marinade, turning it to coat it evenly with the mixture. Cover the bowl with plastic film and let stand at room temperature for 1 hour (or marinate the chicken in the refrigerator for up to 24 hours). Meanwhile, wash and peel the potatoes. Wash and trim the carrots; peel the onions and garlic cloves. Cut the potatoes, carrots and onions into 2.5 cm (1 inch) chunks; crush the garlic cloves; set aside.

Preheat the oven to 200°C (400°F or Mark 6). Combine the vegetables in a large baking dish, sprinkle them with the oil and the remaining salt and pepper, and toss to coat the vegetables with oil. Bake for 30 minutes, or until the potatoes are softened. Add the chicken and marinade to the baking dish and stir to combine. Cover the dish with foil, reduce the oven temperature to 180°C (350°F or Mark 4) and bake for another 30 minutes, or until the chicken is tender. Transfer the chicken and vegetables to a serving dish, sprinkle with coriander and serve.　　　　　　　　　　　　Makes 4 servings

Banana-Blueberry Rice Pudding

Dessert

BANANA-BLUEBERRY RICE PUDDING

Unlike a dish of ice cream, which may contain more than six teaspoons of sugar and 15 grams of fat, this lightly sweetened dessert of fruit and whole grains provides a slow, steady release of carbohydrate energy with a minimum of fat. The rice and bananas are also good sources of potassium and dietary fibre.

CALORIES per serving	225
82% Carbohydrate	48 g
7% Protein	4 g
11% Fat	3 g
CALCIUM	65 mg
IRON	1 mg
SODIUM	45 mg

**125 g (4 oz) brown rice,
  cooked**
17.5 cl (6 fl oz) skimmed milk
4 tablespoons brown sugar
15 g (½ oz) margarine, melted

1 teaspoon ground cinnamon
**300 g (10 oz) fresh or frozen
  blueberries**
3 bananas, peeled and sliced
1 teaspoon wheat germ

Preheat the oven to 180°C (350°F or Mark 4). In a bowl, stir together the rice, milk, sugar, margarine and cinnamon. If using fresh blueberries, wash, dry, and pick them over. Gently fold the bananas and berries into the rice; transfer it to a 20 cm (8 inch) square baking dish. Sprinkle the pudding with wheat germ, cover it with foil and bake for 30 minutes. Let the pudding cool slightly, then divide it among six dessert bowls and serve.   Makes 6 servings

RAISIN-WALNUT BAKED APPLES

Whether part of a well-deserved post-race meal or carried along on a hike, baked apples are a nice change from raw fruit for dessert. Any leftovers make a handy portable breakfast for a busy morning; add the yogurt topping at the last minute.

4 large cooking apples (about 1.1 kg/2 ¼ lb total weight)	4 tablespoons brown sugar
100 g (3½ oz) raisins	2 tablespoons lemon juice
30 g (1 oz) shelled walnuts, coarsely chopped	1 teaspoon ground cinnamon
	12.5 cl (4 fl oz) plain low-fat yogurt

Preheat the oven to 180°C (350°F or Mark 4). Core each apple from the stalk end without cutting through the bottom, and hollow out a good-sized cavity for the filling. Pare a 2.5 cm (1 inch) strip of peel from the circumference of each apple to prevent splitting during baking; set the apples aside.

In a small bowl, stir together the raisins, walnuts, sugar, 1 tablespoon of lemon juice and the cinnamon. Divide the filling among the apples, then place them in a 20 cm (8 inch) square baking tin. Pour 75 cl (1¼ pints) of hot water into the tin and bake the apples for 1 hour, or until they are very tender; remove them from the oven and set aside to cool slightly. Meanwhile, in a small bowl stir together the yogurt and remaining lemon juice. Serve the apples topped with the yogurt mixture. For a portable dessert, wrap the apples in foil while still slightly warm and place them in the refrigerator; refrigerate the yogurt topping in a separate container.   Makes 4 servings

CALORIES per serving	330
81% Carbohydrate	73 g
4% Protein	4 g
15% Fat	6 g
CALCIUM	106 mg
IRON	2 mg
SODIUM	28 mg

RASPBERRY BREAD PUDDING

Basing a dessert on bread, skimmed milk and fruit makes for a treat with a variety of nutritional advantages. Bread is high in carbohydrates and low in fat; skimmed milk is one of the best sources of dietary calcium (none of the mineral is lost when the fat is removed); and the raspberries are an excellent source of vitamin C and provide almost four grams of dietary fibre in a serving of this dessert.

CALORIES per serving	240
75% Carbohydrate	45 g
15% Protein	9 g
10% Fat	3 g
CALCIUM	157 mg
IRON	2 mg
SODIUM	296 mg

250 g (8 oz) bread	1 teaspoon ground cinnamon
55 cl (18 fl oz) skimmed milk	1 teaspoon pure vanilla extract
45 g (1½ oz) brown sugar	350 g (12 oz) fresh or frozen raspberries
2 eggs	

Cut the bread into 2.5 cm (1 inch) cubes and place them in a large bowl. Combine the milk, sugar, eggs, cinnamon and vanilla in a medium-sized bowl and whisk until well blended. Pour the milk mixture over the bread, add the raspberries, and toss gently to combine. Transfer the mixture to a 20 cm (8 inch) round baking dish and cover it with a plate that will rest on top of the pudding. Place a weight (such as a heavy can or a packet of dried beans) on the plate and set aside at room temperature for 30 minutes.

Preheat the oven to 180°C (350°F or Mark 4). Remove the weight and the plate from the pudding, cover the baking dish with foil and bake for 30 minutes. Serve warm or at room temperature.   Makes 6 servings

Creamy Cantaloupe Soda

Snacks and Beverages

CREAMY CANTALOUPE SODA

It is preferable to get carbohydrates from fruits and fruit juices than from the added refined sugar — up to 10 teaspoons — in a can of cola.

CALORIES per serving	80
80% Carbohydrate	17 g
12% Protein	3 g
8% Fat	1 g
CALCIUM	68 mg
IRON	Trace
SODIUM	34 mg

1 cantaloupe melon (about 1 kg/2 lb)
12.5 cl (4 fl oz) plain low-fat yogurt

25 cl (8 fl oz) soda water
3 tablespoons apple juice concentrate
Ice cubes (optional)

Using a melon baller or spoon, scoop the melon into a bowl. Combine the melon, yogurt, soda water and apple juice concentrate in a blender and process on high speed for about 1 minute, or until thick and smooth. Pour into four tall glasses, over ice if desired, and serve. Makes 4 servings

140

CARIBBEAN SHAKE

Keeping your body well hydrated helps ensure the proper functioning of your muscles. Drink lots of water during exercise, and enjoy this cool tropical fruit shake afterwards.

CALORIES per serving	**135**
90% Carbohydrate	32 g
8% Protein	3 g
2% Fat	0.4 g
CALCIUM	97 mg
IRON	Trace
SODIUM	34 mg

One 600 g (20 oz) can juice-packed crushed pineapple, drained

1 banana, peeled and sliced

25 cl (8 fl oz) skimmed milk

25 cl (8 fl oz) ice cubes

½ teaspoon coconut extract

4 mint sprigs

Combine the pineapple, banana, milk, ice cubes and coconut extract in a blender. Blend on high speed for 2 minutes, or until thick and smooth. Pour the shake into four tall glasses, and serve garnished with the mint sprigs.

Makes 4 servings

ONION-CURRY FLATBREAD

In order to maintain a high energy level, replenish your body's glycogen stores by eating carbohydrates within two hours of exercising. A serving of this flatbread will provide 38 grams of carbohydrates.

CALORIES per serving	**205**
71% Carbohydrate	38 g
13% Protein	7 g
16% Fat	4 g
CALCIUM	27 mg
IRON	2 mg
SODIUM	53 mg

1 tablespoon light brown sugar

7 g (¼ oz) dried yeast

350 g (12 oz) wholemeal flour

225 g (7½ oz) plain flour, approximately

250 g (8 oz) red onions

4 garlic cloves

2 tablespoons olive oil

1 teaspoon curry powder

¼ teaspoon salt

¼ teaspoon black pepper

1 egg

In a large bowl, stir together the sugar, yeast and 30 cl (½ pint) of warm water (40-45°C/105-115°F); set aside for 10 minutes. Stir in the wholemeal flour, then add enough of the plain flour to form a soft dough. Turn the dough out on to a lightly floured surface and knead for 10 minutes, kneading in additional plain flour as necessary to make the dough smooth and elastic. Rinse and dry the bowl. Form the dough into a ball, place it in the bowl, cover it with a damp tea towel and set aside to rise in a draught-free place for 1 to 1½ hours, or until doubled in bulk.

Meanwhile, peel the onions and garlic. Thinly slice the onions; crush the garlic. Heat the oil in a large pan over medium heat. Add the onions, garlic, curry powder, salt and pepper, and cook, stirring frequently, for 7 minutes, or until the onions are softened. Remove the pan from the heat and set aside.

Preheat the oven to 230°C (450°F or Mark 8). Lightly oil two large baking sheets. Break the egg into a small bowl and beat it until blended; set aside. Knock back the dough and divide it into six equal pieces; cover them with a tea towel. Place one piece of dough on a lightly floured board and roll it into a 20 by 12.5 cm (8 by 5 inch) rectangle, leaving the edges slightly thicker than the centre. Transfer this piece of dough to a baking sheet and brush it with egg, then top it with onions and garlic. Repeat with the remaining dough. Bake the flatbreads for 15 minutes, or until lightly browned. Allow to cool slightly before serving. Cut the breads in half and serve.

Makes 12 servings

ACKNOWLEDGEMENTS

The editors wish to thank Norma MacMillan.

Nutritional analyses provided by Hill Nutrition Associates, New York State.

Index prepared by Robert Hernandez

PHOTOGRAPHY CREDITS

Exercise photographs © David Madison 1988, except photographs on pages 94-95 © Nancie Battaglia 1985; pages 98-99 © DUOMO/Steven E. Sutton 1985; pages 100-103 © Warren Morgan; page 104 by John Iacono/Sports Illustrated; Food photographs and equipment on pages 24-27 by Steven Mays, Rebus, Inc.

ILLUSTRATION CREDITS

Pages 9, 33, illustrations: Phil Scheuer; pages 10, 13, 18-19, 20-21, 22-23, 106-107, charts: Brian Sisco; pages 14, 44-45, 50-51, 78-79, illustrations: David Flaherty

INDEX